Charging Hell with a Squirt-gun

An Inspirational Instruction For Soul-winners

Charles O. Young, Ph.D.

Charging Hell with a Squirt-gun
An Inspirational Instruction For Soul-winners
by Charles O. Young, Ph.D.

Printed in the United States of America

ISBN 978-0615500805

Table of Contents

Prologue

༒

My future brother-in-law, Gerland, was my 10th grade history teacher in a Christian school in Michigan. Even as a teen and class clown, I noticed Gerland's consistency with his Christian walk. He always seemed to be very steady, never wavering.

Years later when I got out of the service (U.S. Navy), he was still steadily plugging along in his Christian walk. I had little interest in the things of God and used excuses for not attending church. Of course he saw through the excuses and constantly bugged me about getting "into church." His church had just gotten a new pastor and I couldn't think of a good enough excuse NOT to attend so my wife and I began to attend regularly. Little did I know that I was in for the ride of my life. God took hold of my heart during those days, and set my feet on a path that would lead me around the world in Christian service.

"Our" new pastor preached about "soul-winning" but no one in the congregation knew much about it. The church had a regular visitation program with many in the congregation, including myself, partici-pating. Gerland and Jimmy, his friend from church, decided to figure out this "soul-winning" idea and they set out to "win" souls. It wasn't long before they were actively and deliberately sharing the Gospel with lost seekers and leading them to Jesus. Gerland and Jimmy were definitely more excited than the rest of us and I wanted in on it.

I asked Gerland and Jimmy to take me with them when they went soul-winning. They agreed and I spent time with each of them learning what THEY knew about the subject. The day that I was scheduled to go with Jimmy, I had a convicting experience at work. By that time I was a manager of a computer department of a company in Detroit. I had a friend at work who had no idea I was a believer.

Like many immature believers do, I had success-fully hidden my faith, until now. Suddenly it didn't seem right to me that I was going "soul-winning" that night but hadn't even told my colleagues at work that I was a Christian. That day I tried to tell my friend but fell victim to my own fear (once you conquer your own fear, the rest is easy). That night, when I got to Jimmy's, I waited for him in his living room. As I waited, I picked up Jimmy's Bible and randomly opened it to the book of Romans. My eyes fell onto a verse that was underlined, verse 16. To my great embarrassment I read "I am not ashamed of the Gospel of Christ, for it is the power of God unto salvation." OUCH! I had been soundly rebuked.

That night I made a decision to go back to my friend at work AND to all my other friends who did not know that I was a believer, and share with them the "Gospel of Christ." It was a traumatic decision that would change my life and send me on a life-long journey both spiritual and physical. God was working in my life BIG time.

I have formed a very deliberate opinion that I have not changed over the years: soul-winning is the most *valuable* thing that I can possibly do in this life. As I look back over the years I have asked and answered a question provoked by Proverbs 11:30 "... he that wins souls is wise." What comes first, the winning or the wisdom? Perhaps it's the wisdom. It certainly is a wise person that understands the value of a soul. It is also a wise person that considers the vastness of eternity. On the other hand, every soul-winning experience seemed to teach me another truth that would help mold me. Perhaps soul-winning and wisdom feed off each other. At any rate it is the right thing to do.

As of this writing, I have led several thousand people to Jesus. Each of the early chapters in this book tells of a notable soul-winning experience through which I learned some valuable lesson. Maybe you can learn something too. In the later chapters I will deal with some very important considerations regarding soul-winning, namely:

INTENTIONALITY

If we want to be effective in that for which Jesus died, we must fix our minds on "things that are above." It is unlikely that we will ever think about personal evangelism unless we do it on purpose. You must decide on a venue. You must develop a presentation. You must train your mind to think in bridge statements. You must develop a philosophy that creates an evangelist mindset. You must see people as people who once did not exist but will always exist somewhere. You must become accomplished in sharing your own testimony.

BRIDGE STATEMENTS

If asked, most believers could tell someone how to accept Jesus as their Savior. It is also true that most Believers are amicable enough to carry on a regular conversation about the general things of life. The sticking point then becomes how to turn a conversation from the general things of life to the Gospel. It is my opinion that once the subject is changed, the rest is fairly easy. Once the door is opened in a tasteful and sensible way, speaking the Gospel message isn't complicated. Most of the bridge statements that I use regularly were the product of simply keeping my ears opened, listening for a connection.

VENUE

It is not likely that you will consistently win people to Jesus unless you find a venue where you can serve. Don't worry about being comfortable. It has never been about your comfort. I think that God wants us to always be stretching ourselves. Jesus certainly wasn't comfortable at Calvary.

PRESENTATION

As an associate pastor, my job was to ensure that all first time visitors were visited *and* that an aggressive outreach program was implemented. It made sense to me that all people representing the church should be competent to present the gospel. As a matter of procedure, we began a soul-winning class to ensure that those making follow-up visits could make a sensible presentation of the Gospel. Can you do that?

PHILOSOPHY

One advantage of becoming advanced in age is that you have had time to have lots of experiences. This section is about my journey and some of the things that I have learned as well as philosophies that I have formed. These snippets of homespun wisdom will help you on your path to become a strong personal soul-winner.

I have formed the opinion that most Christians are bored with their faith experience. Robert C. Shannon, missionary and religious leader, once made a statement regarding missionaries that I believe applies to any soul-winner. **"Never pity missionaries; envy them. They are where the real action is — where life and death, sin and grace, Heaven and Hell, time and eternity converge."** It doesn't sound boring does it?

If you decide to venture down the pathway of personal evangelism (soul-winning) you can be assured that you will *not* be bored. May God bless you on *your* journey.

Charge

❧

"MOVE OUT AND DRAW FIRE!" U.S. Army Company Commander

When Jesus chose His disciples, He did not seek highly qualified prominent people. Instead he chose common people upon whom to place the burden of spreading the most vital message known to mankind. The message was the message of redemption. The message was the only way to reconcile a sinful world to a Holy God. The question that needs to be answered about that choice is "why?" Why not take the message to the highest points of religion and government? Doesn't it stand to reason that the message would filter down to the masses? Wouldn't you think that such a precious story would become common knowledge if placed into the right hands?

History gives the answer. From the very beginning the message WAS placed with the highest levels of people. Adam had the experience of walking and talking with God. Adam and Eve lived in Utopia. It was a perfect place with every human need supplied straight from the hand of God. Unfortunately, or fortunately, depending on your sovereignty theology, perfection was not enough for our earliest parents. In fact, once human nature was fully developed the world became a very wicked place. It was so wicked in fact that God called Noah to start over. After the flood the message was once again placed into the care of the highest level of existence. It didn't take long for the human race to not only turn their backs on God but also to "become" Gods, through the tower of Babel. Perhaps if God called Abraham to start over again to produce people of faith, the top down approach would work? Maybe Moses could do it! No? Well then, how about creating an entire line of people who would be "priests" of the whole world (Levites)? These Levites (priests) would be the ones who would make the decision to reject the Son of God and crucify Him. None of this is the fault of God. It is simply the natural tendency of man. Man tends to "wind down" in his spiritual intensity.

We know that the tendency of man is to form "religions" which have a way of evolving beyond truth. How many religions do we have in the world anyway? It certainly seems that the top down approach has never worked for long. Just think of the principles upon which the United States of America were founded. How close are we to those principles today as a nation? Are you getting this?

Jesus went to the common people and assigned them the message of the Gospel and charged them to spread it throughout the world. Matthew 28:19-20 says, "Go therefore and make disciples of all the nations, baptizing them in the name of the Father and of the Son and of the Holy Spirit, teaching them to observe all things that I have commanded you; and lo, I am with you always, *even* to the end of the age." In John chapter 1, John testified to Andrew, Andrew to Peter, Andrew and Peter were friends of Philip who believed, Philip found Nathaniel and the chain reaction was started, face to face. Ordinary people telling ordinary people that Jesus is the Messiah, the Son of God. It wasn't a religion; it was personal relationships with Jesus. It was following Jesus to the cross where He would die for the sins of the entire world, giving us an incredible message: we can have a relationship with God through Jesus.

As recorded in Matthew 4:19, when Jesus called Simon and Andrew to leave their fishing careers, He told them "follow me and I will make you fishers of men." As a missionary in Portugal, I worked with a local young woman who had agreed to start a "seeker" Bible study. As word spread throughout her workplace about the Bible study, one coworker came to her and asked "are you fishing for me?" The answer is a resounding YES. Since following Jesus makes one a fisher of men the question must be asked, "If one is not a fisher of men, is he a follower of Jesus?" I think no.

Over the years I have seen lives transformed, homes restored, people start a new life in Christ, many commit to give of their incomes, huge time commitments serving in church on boards or teaching classes, but FEW actually are willing to share the Gospel with a lost person. I have developed an opinion about WHY that disparity exists. I think that people in general make sharing the Gospel too complicated. This book will help make it simpler. Sharing your faith with another has been said to be like "one beggar telling another beggar where to find a handout." It does not have to be confrontational. It's all about choosing words carefully and picking good opportunities. This book is full of stories and illustrations, with techniques that will help you become a true "follower of Jesus."

Early Fruit

❧

"The gospel is only good news if it gets there in time" — Carl F. H. Henry

One day during my earliest memory of soul-winning, I was bored with nothing to do on a Saturday. During the early years of my journey I was in the computer field. At that time I was the Data Processing Manager (IT Manager today) of Detroit Coca-Cola Bottling Company. I was not a "minister", just an impassioned Christian attempting to fulfill the Great Commission.

I went alone to the mall on that Saturday morning for the express purpose of leading someone to Jesus. It was getting close to Christmas and the mall was full of people. I began to scan the mall trying to decide whom to approach. I saw a man sitting in a wheelchair apparently waiting for another shopper to rejoin him. I thought to myself that this man would be too easy to win, so I passed him up. I was looking for more of a challenge (silly me). I have always joked that God takes care of babies and fools and I'm no baby. God seemed to wink at my immaturity.

Suddenly, ***there he was***! I saw the person that I would approach. He was a hippy sort of fellow sitting on the edge of the fountain. I sat down next to him and commenced some small talk. "Is your wife off spending your money?" I asked. He nodded and the encounter was joined. In those days I only knew one opening line to engage the spiritual conversation, "Do you mind if I ask you a spiritual question?" He saw no reason to say no, so I asked the *bomb*, "If you died today would you go to heaven?" He thought a moment and said, "I don't know." I asked him if he would mind if I shared some scriptural truths with him and he agreed.

At that point I reached into my back pocket and pulled out my New Testament. ***WOW!*** You would have thought that I pulled out a snake. He reacted very nervously and said "put that thing away." I did. Fortunately I had the Romans Road to salvation verses memorized (PRESENTATION). I presented the plan of salvation to him in the mall. *The prayer for salvation was a challenge.* People were everywhere walking past within two or three feet. I told him that we needed to approach Jesus through prayer but that it would be a challenge in this noisy place. I encouraged him to bow his head with me and try hard to focus on Jesus. After all, Jesus is the one through whom we pray. We did, he did. **In front of hundreds of people we both bowed our heads and prayed.** I led him in the sinner's prayer, challenging him to be sincere. He prayed along. I wish there were some way of being able to tell immediately if a person is sincere. There is no way. Only God knows.

In a minute his wife showed up and he left. But wait! I noticed a security guard standing over against the wall. He had been watching all the time. He approached me and said, "I saw what you just did......praise the Lord." My boldness level jumped through the ceiling.

I learned first that you should memorize the verses necessary to lead some to Jesus. Secondly, I learned that God truly does take care of babies and fools.

Everyone Needs to Hear

❧

"No one has the right to hear the gospel twice, while there remains someone who has not heard it once." — Oswald J. Smith

In the 70's I belonged to a church where personal evangelism (soul-winning) was often preached. The church put together a class, teaching and enabling our fellow laborers to join in the battle. Many accepted the challenge and the battle for souls was joined.

In Warren, there was a certain housing development where we would go door knocking (hard core soul-winning) each year. One day while in a certain courtyard, we met a man who seemed a little scary to us. He was very gruff and looked quite intimidating. We had developed a certain way to speak to people who answered the doors when we knocked. I held up a tract, moved it toward the door and said in an almost apologetic way "we are just out today inviting people to church". The tract had a schedule of services on the cover with the church name and address. If the person opened the door to take the tract, I would say while opening the tract, "inside it will tell you how to get to heaven when you die; I guess we all care about that don't we?" If they responded in a positive way, I would pull the tract back and say "I am somewhat of a specialist in that area; may I share with you how that works?" At that point they would agree or not.

We were invited into this man's home, which was a bit of a surprise to me based on first impressions. After sharing with him the Romans road (PRESENTATION), and suggesting that we take care of his salvation today, he said that he didn't think that God would save him considering his past behavior and present lifestyle. I asked him if he *wanted* to be saved. He said yes. I asked him *how bad* he wanted to be saved. He felt that it was very important. I suggested that we should get on our knees to show God how sincere he was. He agreed. On our knees he followed me in the sinner's prayer. I wish that I could tell on the spot if a person *got it*. I have never been able to tell. I asked him "did God save you?" He responded that he didn't know.

Something very interesting happened next. He pulled out his wallet and handed me a five dollar bill and asked me to put it into the offering plate the next Sunday. I said that I had a better idea. Why didn't he do it? He agreed to meet me at church the next Sunday and would put the money into the plate. GUESS WHAT? He didn't come.

The next week we went back to see him again. He met us at the door where I asked "are you still saved?" He said that he didn't know but he did have a question for me. He said that he and his friends usually go to the bar for lunch and more or less drink their lunch. Then he asked me "is that the wrong thing to do?" WOW! A spiritual thought, something that he had never wondered before. I immediately concluded that he HAD gotten saved and that he was now being convicted by the Holy Spirit about his lifestyle. Praise the Lord! He ***got it***.

I learned a couple of things from this encounter (1) never judge who should hear a presentation (2) if you want them to go to church, pick them up (3) take the money.

Divine Providence

"Any church that is not seriously involved in helping fulfill the Great Commission has forfeited its biblical right to exist." — Oswald J. Smith

My wife, children and I had just moved into an apartment near Tampa. We were only to stay there until we could learn the area and find permanent housing. In the apartment next to ours was a family of three, husband, wife and adolescent daughter - Jack, Jill and Julie (not their real names). Julie was near the age of our children. We were cordial with the family, waving and making small talk when we ran into them.

We settled into a church quickly and asked the little girl if she would like to go to Sunday school with us (INTENTIONALITY, VENUE). Her family liked the idea and she accompanied us to church the next Sunday. Upon arriving home we walked the new friend to the door and were met by the parents.

They asked if she liked the experience and she said that she did.

By this point in my soul-winning journey, I had grown more interested in finding "*fruit that remains*" John 15:16. I saw the value of working with someone until they could stand on their own two "spiritual" feet. I said to the parents that I knew that every parent wanted to know what their kids were taught in Sunday school (BRIDGE STATEMENTS), and I asked them if I could stop by on Monday evening for a briefing; they agreed. It turned out that they were what I call **"low hanging fruit."** They were quite ready to accept Jesus as their Savior and they did. I offered to come to their apartment every Monday and teach them a 10 lesson series that I had developed to help them grow in the Lord. We began the next week.

The lessons taught them about basic Christian practices - Bible reading, prayer, baptism, church attendance (they began attending our church), giving, and witnessing. When we did the lesson on prayer, I asked them if they had someone that they wanted to pray for to accept Jesus. *Jack's brother was the main candidate.* When we got to lesson 10, we discussed that *God wants us to share our faith with others.* I suggested that we set up a time and go visit his brother. We did. After we explained to the brother that Jack had accepted Jesus, we discussed what that meant and the brother followed suit. He too accepted Jesus. Soon thereafter both of our families moved out of the apartment complex and we lost track of each other. It would be 10 years before we would see them again.

Fast forward 10 years. I had a suit that I kept for funerals and weddings. I hadn't worn it for a while and decided to get it cleaned. It needed to be let out some to accommodate my urban spread (I had gained weight). I had just picked the suit up from the cleaners and was bringing it in from the car when my wife met me on the porch with the phone in her hand. It was Jack. The brother that we led to the Lord had just died suddenly. I was shocked, knowing that he was only in his 40's. They asked me to do the funeral. There I stood with my burying suit in my hand that I had just gotten altered and cleaned. *It still gives me chills thinking about the convergence of circumstances.*

I had to relearn about the brother. It seems that he had turned out to be a pretty good Christian, very active in church and rather influential among his fellows. The funeral was packed with perhaps 200 people. I gave my evangelistic funeral presentation. Every time that I looked at Jill during the sermon, she was choking back tears. She knew that all of those people were hearing the Gospel. It was all that I could do not to break down too. Some two dozen people accepted Jesus that day at the funeral. Praise the Lord!

Why did I choose to have my suit altered and cleaned at that time? Do you know? How much of this story do you think is providential (directed by God)? Was it providential that: We moved to Tampa? We took an apartment next to theirs? We invited the daughter to church? I was obedient in sharing the Gospel? We were led to direct them to personal witnessing? We went to the brother's home? I got my suit fixed? Two dozen accepted Jesus? You are reading this article?

The Judge and the Guilty

꧁꧂

"As long as there are millions destitute of
the Word of God and knowledge of Jesus
Christ, it will be impossible for me to
devote time and energy to those who have
both." — J. L. Ewen

In the year 2000 I began serving as a corporate
chaplain (VENUE). I was assigned 6 companies
with about 700 employees total, to visit each week.
My task was to speak to each employee at least once
a week to check and see if they needed some confi-
dential help. It was a most fruitful ministry, allowing
me to lead 650 to Jesus in 5 years.

One of my earlier encounters was visiting a man
- whom we'll call "Bill" - in jail who had violated his
probation for domestic violence and driving under the
influence. When I first saw him in jail he was a sight
- eyes blood-shot, hair disheveled, and quite groggy
looking. In his desperate condition, he said that his
problem all boiled down to alcohol. I responded that
perhaps he had not boiled it down far enough. "Let's

just call it sin," I said. He agreed. I told him that sin is processed differently than alcohol. In just a few minutes he accepted Jesus as his Savior. That was the easy beginning to a very difficult journey.

I immediately recommended that he bond out of jail and admit himself to a Christian rehab program. Perhaps when he got to court, the judge would see that he was trying to do the right thing and show some leniency by sentencing him to that same rehab program. I don't mind saying that the program is called Teen Challenge, a program that has grown to include men and women, as well as teens with addiction problems. Teen Challenge is a Pentecostal program that was born several decades ago in New York City. I lament the fact that the Pentecostals are the only people who are willing to dip down to help these kinds of people. Other denominational groups have managed to keep their hands cleaner. I strongly recommend Teen Challenge.

Since his crimes included several counts and breaking parole for more than one offense, Bill had to appear before two different judges. Each time Bill had a court date I had to get up at four in the morning, drive to the facility to pick him up, go with him to court, and drive him back to the facility. The state's attorney was asking for 10 years in jail for the many repeated offenses. I took him to court at least nine times over the next several months, until the final hearing in each court.

On the final day in the family court (domestic violence) I stood up for him before the judge. I asked the court to sentence him to as much time as thought necessary at Teen Challenge. He needed his "brains washed" to help him think differently. His old ways must be changed from his heart out. As I stood before the judge I began to feel like Jesus must feel, standing between the judge and the guilty. Pretty good theology, huh? The judge agreed with me and gave the sentencing for him to remain in Teen Challenge. This was one court down and one to go.

In the last court, Bill and I were advised that it was very unlikely that the judge would bend from the recommended state sentencing guidelines, 10 years. Once again I stood between the judge and the guilty. My emotions were running high. It was obvious that I was heavily invested in this man's life. To the surprise of all, the judge took my recommendation and sentenced Bill to two years at Teen Challenge. Even now, seven years later, I get emotional thinking and writing about this.

Through this experience, I learned things about Jesus in my heart that I had only known in my head. I John 2:1, "if any man sin, we have an advocate with the Father, Jesus Christ the Righteous."

"For God to reveal His Son in us is not the result of research or searching; it is entirely a matter of mercy and revelation. It is an inward seeing, an inner knowing."— Watchman Nee

Shared Prayer

"When I pray, coincidences happen, and when I don't pray, they don't." —William Temple

My wife, Jeanette, was searching for a new hairdresser. Someone recommended a certain salon to her in Birmingham, Michigan. While there she met the owner, a nice man with whom she began to share her excitement about our home church. He showed some interest and they struck up a cordial friendship. Every time she went into the shop, they would re-engage about the church. As a couple, we were invited to a social gathering where we connected with him and his wife (let's call them Bill and Sue). Jeanette and I did not see them much, but for some reason we became rather fond of them as a couple. We didn't speak together about them, but they seemed to be in our minds. A year went by without us seeing them or even talking about them.

One Sunday evening at church, Jeanette and I responded to the sermon which challenged us to have a daily family prayer time. We made the commitment to pray together daily. *That one thing has been a real struggle for us over the years.* We never officially stopped doing it but we have restarted many times. Our individual pace and temperament have made shared prayer a struggle for us. As easy as it sounds and as beneficial as it is, I regret that we have been largely unsuccessful in that practice.

On the next Monday morning, after our Sunday evening commitment, we met together to pray before we both went to work. As we bowed our heads, I let Jeanette lead out in prayer. While she was praying aloud, I was praying silently. For some reason Bill and Sue were in my mind, and I was praying for them to become Christians. *Imagine my surprise when I heard my wife pray for Bill and Sue.* **Hey! I was also praying for them.** When it became my turn to pray out loud, I too prayed for Bill and Sue. Both Jeanette and I shed tears for them that morning. When the prayer time was over I suggested that if we were going to pray for them, we should go see them. We both agreed. We decided to drop by their house the next Thursday evening. We went unannounced in order not to create any anxiety or questions about our visit.

When we got there, we were welcomed into their home. They were always very cordial people. We began by telling them that we were concerned for them and wanted to share with them our faith. They already knew that we were very active in our church. I gave them the plan of salvation (PRESENTATION). It was accompanied by tears from Jeanette and me.

At the end of my presentation, I suggested that we "take care of this matter." Sue began to share with us an inner desire to know God. She told us that just the other day she had said to Bill, "I think that we should become Christians." My wife immediately wanted to know when that was. Sue said "Monday morning." (Give me a here minute to wipe the tears from my eyes.) *Monday morning!* That was when Jeanette and I had prayed together for them. That was when God put it into their hearts. They both bowed their heads and accepted Jesus as their Savior.

I learned two things that day of which I have been reminded many, many times over the years. First, I learned the truth of Psalm 126:6 "He that goes forth weeping bearing precious seed will doubtless come again with rejoicing, bringing his sheaves with him." *I have since coined that the soul-winner's guarantee.* The second truth that I learned was from Matthew 18:19 "…. If two of you shall agree on earth as touching anything that they shall ask, it shall be done for them of my Father which is in heaven". The agreement that my wife and I had was not a stated agreement in principle but was a mutual burden of heart. My best guess is that God put it there.

The Plans of God

❦

"The purposes of God point to one simple end—that we should be as he is, think the same thoughts, mean the same things, and possess the same blessedness." –George MacDonald

During some door-to-door visitation (VENUE), my partner and I encountered a rather old gentleman, in his 90's. He invited us into his house which was a bit dark, dank and smelled a bit like old man. (Since then I have begun to smell like that.) He was very nice to us and was willing to hear what we had to say about salvation. The gentleman was somewhat hard of hearing but we managed to be able to communicate. He told us that he was not a follower of Jesus. The operative question in those days was, "If you were to die tonight would you go to heaven?" He did not know nor did he know how to know.

He did tell us that his son was a missionary in Africa. When I was a teen my family went to a church in the same town where we were doing our visiting.

Once a month my mother would go to a meeting at church called a "missionary circle." Each group or "circle" was assigned a missionary with whom they would communicate on a regular basis. The "circle" would try to meet the needs of the missionary as best they could. It just so happened that this old gentleman was the father of the missionary my mother served for years. The missionary had been in Africa for 30 years. Upon our visit to the older gentleman's house, I quickly put it together in my mind that this was our famous missionary's father. I was amazed by this "coincidence."

I had some strange feelings about this experience while I was in this house. At first I wondered how this missionary could leave his father "lost" and go to a foreign country to win the "lost." In my heart I became a little indignant. "I" would take care of this missionary's business for him while he ignored his own father. Years later I have changed my mind about the whole thing. I have concluded that the only perfect time to serve God is *now*. If you commit to take care of God's business, *God will take care of yours*. The old man opened his heart to Jesus that night. **What a blessing!**

Sometime later the old man died. I can't remember how I learned about the death but I determined to go to the funeral. At the funeral I met the missionary for the very first time. I was stunned to hear him speak. *He stuttered uncontrollably.* Imagine, a person that God chose to preach the Gospel couldn't speak a sentence without this terrible distraction. It helped me learn the truth of I Corinthians 1:27 ".. God has chosen the foolish things of the world to confound the wise; and God has chosen the weak things of the world to confound the things which are mighty." I felt very humble to be in the presence of this man of God.

Having led that now deceased gentleman to the Lord, I experienced several emotions as the funeral was conducted, self satisfaction, arrogance, and pride, which were overpowered by humility, respect and a bit of awe, Isaiah 55:8-9 "For my thoughts are not your thoughts, neither are your ways my ways, says the Lord. For as the heavens are higher than the earth, so are my ways higher than your ways, and my thoughts than your thoughts." In the lofty plan of God I was only the smallest piece in a giant puzzle.

The Holy Spirit

❧

"Many people have come to Christ as a result of my participation in presenting the Gospel to them. It's all the work of the Holy Spirit." - Billy Graham

I never did like going door to door. It was very hard core, required quick thinking, was somewhat traumatic but was always fruitful. It seemed like someone always accepted Jesus when we endured our discomfort and went door to door. One year when I was an associate pastor in charge of outreach, we purposed to knock on every door within 50 square miles surrounding our church. We did not merely hand out church bulletins; we had tracts in one hand and New Testaments in the other. We trained our church members on what to say, and they said it. Five specific times were set for soul-winning during the week, and it was constantly preached from the pulpit. Several thousand people accepted Jesus that year and we baptized over 800. Our church attendance went from 200 to 1500 in three years. **To God be the glory!**

One day, while standing at a lady's door sharing my faith, I launched into an illustration to help her understand making a commitment to Jesus. Each time this sort of thing happened to me some marvelous ideas came out of my mouth. I truly had no idea where this was going and I was listening as closely as she was. **I didn't want to miss anything.** The idea of commitment went something like this: I was in the military during the late 60's while Vietnam was in full play. At the end of boot camp, some went on to further training to learn how to jump out of airplanes. The teachers would put you into a classroom and teach you all about parachutes. They would draw one on the black board showing the technical aspects of parachutes. Then they would bring one into the classroom and let you become familiar with its feel. You could tug on the straps, pull on the cords and generally become confident in the mechanics of the parachute. I liken this to religion, sitting in a classroom, learning about that which would someday become your savior. *But learning was not enough.* Finally came the day. With parachute strapped to your back, up you would go in the airplane. So far, all you had learned was theory. Standing in the door of the plane at several thousand feet in the air, all would become a reality. **Geronimo!** The next step was where you actually put your trust in the parachute. With Jesus it is when you open your heart to Him, taking a leap of faith, and calling unto Him to save your soul (Romans 10:13 "whosoever shall call upon the name of the Lord, shall be saved.") The lady on the porch said, "For the first time, I think I understand." *She took the plunge.*

I have learned the truth of Matthew 28:20 as I've been busy about the Great Commission - "Lo, I am with you always." Most of the bridge statements and illustrations that I use while winning people to Jesus have come in the heat of battle, contending for men's souls. Acts 1:8 says, "You shall receive power after the Holy Ghost is come upon you, and you shall be witnesses." My part in soul-winning is *obedience*, His part is the saving.

"The work of the Spirit is to impart life, to implant hope, to give liberty, to testify of Christ, to guide us into all truth, to teach us all things, to comfort the believer, and to convict the world of sin." - Dwight L. Moody

Never Judge

~~~~

"Plant a word in the mind, and you will reap an act. Plant the act and you will reap a habit. Plant a habit and you will reap a character. Plant a character and you will reap a nature. Plant a nature and you will reap a destiny." - Unknown

As a senior pastor, I was visited in my office one day by a salesman. (Let's call him Bill.) I politely listened to his proposal but did not have any interest in his program. At the end of his presentation, I told him that I too had a presentation and thought it would be fair for him to listen to mine. He agreed. I presented to him the plan of salvation. It turned out that I was better at closing the deal then he was (PRESENTATION). We bowed our heads together and I led him in the sinner's prayer. He prayed along with me. When the prayer was over, I remember the thought crossing my mind that he was only patronizing me. I thought that he was not sincere and probably did not truly accept Jesus.

The next day he called me on the phone. He told me that he was concerned about his aging grandmother and wondered if I would go to his house and meet with her, sharing my faith like I did with him. I agreed. (It started to look like he may have been sincere after all.) When I got to his house it seems that he was concerned for his entire family. He sat me down at his kitchen table and brought in all of his family, including his grandmother, father, mother, two brothers and a sister. They all joined me at the table. Well! This caught me quite by surprise. I began to cordially interact with the family, chatting around the table with each person. Bill would have none of that. He placed a Bible in front of me saying, "Tell them what you told me yesterday." I did share with them all the plan of salvation. Each person bowed their heads with me, accepting Jesus as their savior. They all began to come to my church.

That does not end the story. Bill began a practice of calling me from time to time saying that he had a "live one" and asking me to meet him for lunch to help him lead a friend to Jesus. We did this several times. He had witnessed to them to the point where they were all but saved. I had very little to do with their salvation. Bill had already made his testimony known to them.

That does not end the story. One day Bill called me to ask me if I would come to his office. He was doing a training session with some new people in his company and had been witnessing to them. He asked if I would come to help him lead them to Jesus. I certainly agreed. When I got to his office there were six newbies sitting around the conference table. Bill put me in his office behind his desk and, one by one, sent each trainee into the office where I could lead them to Jesus. All six accepted Jesus.

I will never again judge who actually receives Jesus. I have no way of telling, but I feel sure that Bill did. What do you think? It makes sense to me that if one truly accepts Jesus as his Savior that he would want to share that with his family. Mark 5:19 says, *"Go home to your friends, and tell them what great things the Lord has done for you, and how He has had compassion on you."*

Surprise

❦

"Unless you have made a complete surrender and are doing His will it will avail you nothing if you've reformed a thousand times and have your name on fifty church records." - <u>Billy Sunday</u>

I was asked to preach at a banquet supporting the bus ministry in the late 1970's. During those days, gas was cheap and old used buses were cheaper. The bus ministry was my first entry into the ministry. My wife and I picked up 100 kids a week and brought them to church. On Tuesday and Thursday evenings, we would go back into the homes and share our faith with the parents. Dozens of parents and more kids accepted Jesus. Regarding the banquet, I began to pray that God would give me an appropriate message and a fresh personal evangelism illustration with which to inspire the workers serving in the bus ministry.

As a pastor I always practiced, taught and preached "soul-winning." There was a young man (let's call him Dennis) in my church that became inspired during one Sunday message and asked if he could go with me the next time that I went out. I agreed and we set up a time for a trip to the battle-field. Our prescribed time for the meeting was the next Tuesday morning. Spot on time Dennis showed up. I had actually forgotten about the date and was caught unprepared with no place to go. On the spur of the moment, I grabbed some Gospel tracts and we set out to canvass a neighborhood (VENUE).

As we went door to door we met people, engaging them in conversation and sharing our faith. We came to one house and met an older lady who was very cordial and allowed us to discuss matters of faith with her. Early on she mentioned that she had an old uncle that was a minister who had died years ago. It didn't interest me much so I didn't ask her much about him. I did ask her if she were to die would she go to Heaven. She said that she thought she would. I asked her why and she told me that she made cakes for the neighbor and everyone thought well of her. A bit taken aback by her answer, I asked her if she ever made a cake for God. "Of course not" she replied. I told her that the cakes for her neighbors were very nice and pleased her neighbors but it took something else to please God. At this thought she invited us in to hear more.

We had just begun to give the plan of salvation (PRESENTATION), when a house keeper showed up. The interruption caused me to stop with the presenta-tion and try to include the housekeeper in the discus-sion. The two of them listened as I shared the Gospel and agreed that it was something important enough to settle today. I suggested that we bow our heads and tell Jesus about the newfound need, inviting Him into their lives, trusting Him as their Savior. The housekeeper asked me to wait for a minute while she made some preparation for prayer. Apparently this young lady had already felt a spiritual need and had mailed in to a radio program for some "anointing oil." She went to her car to fetch the oil and brought it back into the house. After offering some to Dennis and me, (we declined), she applied it liberally to her own hands. Sitting with her opened hands facing up, she announced that she was ready for prayer. We all prayed together and both of my new friends accepted Jesus as their Savior. PTL!

The lady of the house still wanted to talk about her old evangelist uncle. She said to me, "Have you ever heard of Billy Sunday." NO WAY! I had just led Billy Sunday's niece to Jesus. For those of you who don't know, Billy Sunday was a very vocal and powerful evangelist during the time of Prohibition in this country. Try Googling Billy Sunday to find out more about him.

I had my fresh story for the banquet message. God is good!

Family

John 1:41 "He first found his own brother Simon, and said unto him, We have found the Messiah, which is, being interpreted, the Christ and he brought him to Jesus."

My wife Jeanette and I were actively involved in outreach through our church (VENUE). Almost weekly someone was accepting Jesus as their Savior through our efforts. I began to be under conviction about my own lost family member. My brother, even though he went to the same Christian high school I did, had never opened his heart to Jesus. I felt a bit hypocritical trying to win others to Jesus but ignoring my own brother. I realize that "family" is often more difficult for us to approach. In fact Jesus said that "A **prophet** is not without honor, but in his own country, and among his own kin, and in his own house" Mark 6:4 (family, neighborhood, and workplace). I suppose that we are more known by our "context" than we are by our inner interests.

I decided to try to have lunch with my brother and open a dialogue about spiritual things. We met the next week and I began to speak to him about my concern for his spiritual wellbeing. At the end of my prepared speech, he told me that perhaps he would go to church the next Sunday. I have learned over the years that those statements usually mean nothing. However, with the door slightly opened by him, I quickly devised a plan. I told him that I had to be at church early that next Sunday but my wife did not. I asked him if he would mind stopping by and picking up my wife on his way to church. ***Cornered!*** After some brief thought, he agreed. *The plan was afoot.*

That Sunday I went early to church as scheduled and he actually did stop by and pick up my wife. The plan fell apart when my brother dropped off my wife and went out for breakfast alone. ***Oh well! Nice try.***

I sang in the choir in those days and as I sat in the back row of the choir, I was watching some teens that were sitting in the back of the church. I had led them to Jesus that week while visiting in a local neighborhood. I told them that they should meet me at the front during the invitation at the conclusion of the service. This act of public profession would allow other believers to share in their happy experience. As the congregation stood for the invitation I expected them to file out and meet me at the front. They did not move. I tried to beckon to them but was ignored. Perhaps if I stepped out and walked to the front, they would see me moving out and do the same. As I moved to the front row of the church, they did not join me. While standing in the front row, I kept trying to look back at them to see if I could get their attention. I looked around but my view was blocked by someone standing in front of me. **IT WAS MY BROTHER!** Without hearing the sermon, the invitation or even one song, he was walking down the aisle to give himself to Jesus. He had come back to the church after breakfast and walked in just in time for the invitation. We spent some glorious moments kneeling at the altar as he trusted Christ.

Upon reflection, I thought that I had devised a good plan to get my brother under the sound of the Gospel. It turned out that while I was working on his ears, *God was working on his heart*. I realize today that I must do my part to see people come to Jesus but that my part is by far *the smallest part*. I can't reach the heart. **Only God can.**

Isaiah 55:8 **"My thoughts are not your thoughts, neither are your ways my ways, says the LORD."**

Fruit That Remains

❧

"You did not choose Me, but I chose you and appointed you that you should go and bear fruit, and *that* your fruit should remain, that whatever you ask the Father in My name He may give you." John 15:16

As a pastor I was always eager to have new people in my church. An older couple who attended services with fair regularity decided to bring their twenty-something son to church with them. I was familiar with the family but didn't know that they had a son Jim who didn't attend church. Jim showed up one Sunday to my great pleasure.

As was my custom I went the next week to visit the young man in his parents' home. Jim lived with his new wife in their own home, but was at his parents' house that day. I remember the visit as if it were yesterday. Jims' father didn't want me to present the Gospel to Jim. In fact every time I started down the Gospel road, the father would head me off. I distinctly remember him saying more than once,

"He's a good boy." I tried several times to create a dialogue with the young man but was prevented by the dad.

Finally I left the home and purposed to see the son in another venue. Jim owned a small shoe store and I made an appointment to meet him there on a particular day when business was generally slow. As we visited on that day about the matter of salvation, Jim opened his heart to Jesus. It was not a difficult presentation because of his upbringing and his background. I didn't know why he had never accepted Jesus as his Savior before that day. It may have had something to do with his father's protective attitude.

The next challenge was Jim's wife, Sharon. Jim told me that it would be a challenge because his wife was brought up in an active Lutheran home. She was active as a teen and was even a youth leader of some sort. I made an appointment and had my visit with her. Because of her long religious history, she insisted that she was a believer. She told me "I have always believed" (PHILOSOPHY). The more I pressed the matter, the more I was convinced that she had never been born again. It seemed to her that having been that religious all of her life, she must surely be a believer. During her religious upbringing, she went through every step of her religious requirement. She took every course and followed every teaching of her church. I am afraid many people follow the religious practices of their church, assuming that "religious practices" are sufficient for salvation. That was the problem with the salvation of Nicodemus in John 3.

He was all about religion. Jesus told him "you must be born again" (John 3:3).

I was having a difficult time convincing her that she was religious but lost. In Romans 13:11 we are told about a time "*when* we believed." My question to her was "*when* did you believe?" I took her on a quick historic journey through scripture, talking hypothetically to Bible characters asking them when they believed. Zacchaeus said "I was up a tree trying to see Jesus. I knew that they claimed that he was the Messiah and I wanted to see for myself. Jesus stopped at the bottom of the tree and said 'Zacchaeus come down for I am going to your house today.' My heart pounded within my breast as I knew that this WAS the Messiah. That's when I believed." The thief on the cross said, "I was hanging on the cross next to Jesus. Somehow I felt that this was a just man but more, He was the Son of God, the Messiah. That was when I believed." The Ethiopian eunuch said, "I was riding along in a chariot trying to read the Bible when a guy named Philip suddenly showed up. He asked me if I understood what I was reading and I said, NO. He explained to me that the scripture I was reading was talking about Jesus, the Messiah. A brilliant light came on in my heart and suddenly I believed."

I then turned to Sharon and asked her to tell me "*when* did you believe?" She could not tell me of an experience in her life that matched any such experience mentioned in Scripture. I told her that I was trying to make her doubt that the religious experience was sufficient for salvation, that it could replace a SPIRITUAL experience. With a tear in her eye and a quiver in her voice she told me that she "doubted." We bowed our heads and she prayed along with me opening her heart to Jesus, NOT trusting religion.

As time went on Jim and Sharon grew rapidly in the Lord. They both became very active in our church. On Tuesdays Jim would take the morning off from his shoe store and go visiting with me. I didn't know it but on Tuesdays Jim would abstain from smoking (a nasty habit) so as to not disrespect me. I didn't know until years later that he even smoked. Jim went off to Bible college and today is pastoring a church in the Midwest with his faithful wife by his side.. They are some of the bright spots in my evangelistic career. They are "fruit that remains" John 15:16.

Hide the Wallet

꿨

**"But sanctify the Lord God in your hearts,
and always *be* ready to *give* a defense to
everyone who asks you a reason for the
hope that is in you, with meekness and
fear." I Peter 3:15**

As a corporate chaplain I always freely gave out
my business card inviting employees to call me
if they needed help. One Saturday I received a phone
call from a man that I did not know. He was NOT an
employee of any of my client companies. He told me
that he had just gotten out of jail and was standing by
the payphone trying to figure out what to do. He was
new to the area and really did not have anyone whom
he could call for help. Someone walked by him and
handed him one of my business cards and told him
"this guy will help you." I never learned who gave
him the card.

Johnny called me and told me some of his story.
He told me that he had just gotten out of jail and had
no place to turn. I agreed to go pick him up. On the

way to pick up Johnny, I began to realize that I knew nothing about this man and that I was driving blind into a potentially bad situation. As I continued down the road, I felt a little nervous. I called my wife on my cell phone and got voice mail. I left a message something like this: "I have been call to assist a man that I do not know. If you never hear from me again, just know that I was trying to help another human being." I took the wallet out of my pocket and hid it in the car. I put my debit card in my shirt pocket and proceeded down the road. It seemed to me that a person just released from jail could be capable of almost anything.

I picked up Johnny and asked him if he had eaten recently. He said no. I took him to a restaurant and we both had breakfast. Over our meal Johnny told me his sad story of drug abuse and his having spent 90 days in jail. Johnny explained to me that he had asked for a Bible and had spent most of his time reading it during his incarceration. I felt a bit like Philip in Acts 8 as he encountered the Ethiopian eunuch. Philip asked the Ethiopian if he understood what he was reading. The Eunuch answered him, "How can I except some man guide me?" Apparently Johnny was trying to find answers in the Bible. He wanted God to help him and couldn't figure out how to reach God.

I spent the next 30 minutes explaining how one makes that spiritual connection. Johnny watched me closely as I explained. He hung on every word. I felt that he truly wanted to find a relationship with God. The path Johnny was on had landed him in jail. He needed a better way. That day he found out that Jesus said "I am the way." Johnny eagerly accepted Jesus at the breakfast table on that busy Saturday morning.

There we sat full of food and full of Jesus. However, Johnny had no place to stay, no money, no friends and no job. Johnny had told me that he had experience as a mechanic. I quickly thought of one of my company owners for whom I chaplained who might need a mechanic. From the breakfast table I called the owner. He said he would see Johnny the next Monday morning.

That seemed promising. I then called a foreman from that same company who lived by himself and asked him if he could extend a helping hand for a few days. He agreed. I took Johnny directly to that home where he was welcomed with opened arms. Johnny was given a job two days later.

Imagine how Johnny's life improved within the two hours that I spent with him. Johnny went from a prisoner, homeless, helpless, penniless, friendless, jobless, hungry and hopeless to full, housed, with new friends, a job and best of all, an eternal destiny in heaven and a friend that sticks closer than a brother, Jesus.

Jesus said in Matthew 25, *"35 for I was hungry and you gave Me food; I was thirsty and you gave Me drink; I was a stranger and you took Me in; 36 I was naked and you clothed Me; I was sick and you visited Me; I was in prison and you came to Me.' 37 "Then the righteous will answer Him, saying, 'Lord, when did we see You hungry and feed You, or thirsty and give You drink? 38 When did we see You a stranger*

and take You in, or naked and clothe You? 39 Or when did we see You sick, or in prison, and come to You?' 40 And the King will answer and say to them, 'Assuredly, I say to you, inasmuch as you did it to one of the least of these My brethren, you did it to Me.'"
It has been my long desire to be an extension of Jesus. That day I was.

I got back into my car, put my wallet back into my pocket called my wife and told her that I was on my way home.

They are Killing Me

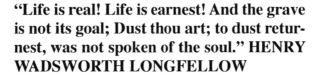

"Life is real! Life is earnest! And the grave is not its goal; Dust thou art; to dust returnest, was not spoken of the soul." HENRY WADSWORTH LONGFELLOW

As a corporate chaplain my responsibility was to visit each employee at least once each week for the purpose of building a relationship and gaining credibility with the employee. It was not a particularly daunting task for I would usually spend only a minute or two with each employee. Some employees were a bit standoffish while others eagerly accepted my visit. James was sort of in the middle. He would accept my weekly greeting but never said anything more than superficial conversation.

One day I was told by the company president that James had been arrested and was in jail. The whole thing seemed out of character for James as he was always conscientious about his work and attendance and was considered quite reliable. Something happened over the weekend and James was arrested for drunkenness and domestic violence toward his wife. I asked the company president if he wanted to reach out to James and bail him out of jail. He agreed, stating that James was a good employee and that he wanted to help him. Then the president asked me how I would use the circumstances to a spiritual advantage. I told him that if I went and bailed James out of jail that then James would "owe" me a little more depth in our conversations.

I drove to another county where James was in jail and went to the appropriate office and paid for James to be bonded out of jail. The whole thing took me an entire afternoon. I didn't see James that day because once bond is paid a prisoner could be released anytime during the next 24 hours.

The next time that I went to the company, I saw James who was more than grateful. He thanked me profusely for my part in helping him get out of jail. I asked him if we could speak in private about the matter and he agreed. We went into the conference room of the business and sat together for about an hour. Apparently James' regular weekend activity included getting drunk. While drunk he said that he was told that he had been violent toward his wife and disabled stepson. He did not remember any of it. He only remembered waking up in jail. Since he did not have a history of such violence, James doubted that he had done anything at all. He felt that his wife and stepson had concocted the entire thing as a plot to get him out of the house and take all that he had. I had no way of knowing the real truth. James kept saying, "They are killing me," as a result of the immense pressure that he felt over the whole incident. His blood pressure was through the roof.

I told James my "three legged stool" illustration (PRESENTATION), and he accepted Jesus as his savior. The court matter was not over because he still needed to stand trial for the accusations. I promised him that I would stand with him. Once again he was grateful. Over the next few weeks, every time that I visited James he would say again, "They are killing me." Well guess what! Within a month he was dead. One weekend he had a massive heart attack and died.

James' fellow workers were shaken by the whole series of events. Within a few days of James' death, all of the workers were invited to come to a brief meeting conducted by me. I spent the time talking very directly about James, his problems (everyone knew) and his having accepted Jesus as his Savior. I have found that when an employee dies then others begin to discuss his eternal destiny. Everybody seems to have their own opinions about those matters at times like that. Using the Bible I cleared up the matter for them. At the same time, I invited all of those present to accept Jesus as James had. That day about a dozen employees responded, opening their hearts to Jesus.

Shortly after James died, I contacted the family and discussed the same matter with them, assuring them that James had accepted Jesus. I was invited to do the funeral and another dozen or so people accepted Jesus, including some family members.

In the Book of Ecclesiastes Chapter 7, we are told "1 A good name *is* better than precious ointment, And the day of death than the day of one's birth; 2 Better to go to the house of mourning Than to go to the house of feasting, For that *is* the end of all men; And the living will take *it* to heart. 3 Sorrow *is* better than laughter, for by a sad countenance the heart is made better. 4 The heart of the wise *is* in the house of mourning, but the heart of fools *is* in the house of mirth."

How can the day of death be better than the day of birth? If one knows Jesus, the day of his death ushers him into the land of peace, the home of the redeemed, into the place without sin, a place where no-one does you wrong, into the presence of perfect Love. The opposite is true of the day of one's birth. Is James in the better place? You bet!

Does it Make Sense

"Whatever your hand finds to do, do *it* with your might; for *there is* no work or device or knowledge or wisdom in the grave where you are going" Ecclesiastes 9:10

My daughter was a nurse on the night shift of a local hospital. One Sunday evening she called me to ask if I could go to the hospital and minister to a family who was seeking help. Their loved one, Phil, was in a coma and dying. When I arrived I met the family and they took me to the room. I saw Phil through the door, lying in the bed all wired up with monitors and medical devices. Phil was dying of AIDS. I didn't ask how Phil got AIDS because it didn't seem very important at that moment.

The wife (or girlfriend, not sure which) asked me to go into the room and "Do whatever it takes to make sure that he goes to Heaven." I looked at the faces of the family members and saw a bit of desperation. They may have seen the same of my face. I have never felt so unqualified in all of my life. Sending someone to heaven is over my pay grade. I quickly tried to think of what to do. Should I tell them that it doesn't work that way? Should I tell them that I couldn't do it?

I suddenly remembered that some people who are in a coma can still hear what's going on around them. I told them that I would do my best and asked everyone to leave me alone with Phil for a few minutes. They did. I sat next to Phil and leaned into his ear and began to talk to him. I told him who I was and that I wanted to speak to him for a few minutes. Then I said something that I had never said or even thought of before. I said "Phil, you are about to meet God, and if you can understand me, I will try to tell you how to make it a pleasant meeting." In the next few minutes I explained to him the "plan of salvation" (PRESENTATION). At the end of the explanation, I led him in a prayer, helping him to ask Jesus to be his Savior. There he lay hours from death but I had done my best. Perhaps God extended mercy to him that day and allowed him to respond to the Gospel. I will know someday.

As I went out of the room, I knew that I must spend some time with the family and share the Gospel with them. The words came to me easily as I said that I wanted to "tell them what I told Phil." We found our way to the cafeteria which was closed and dark because of the lateness of the hour. I gave them the Gospel, explaining that this was what I told Phil. Then I asked them, "Doesn't it make sense to you that you would want to take care of this BEFORE you find yourself in a coma?" They agreed. In fact two of the sons talked for a few minutes and said that this was the first time that this whole thing had made sense to them. That night all four family members accepted Jesus as their Savior. I didn't give them false hope nor did I take away their hope for Phil. I had no way of knowing if Phil had responded. Before I left them that night, I prayed for them and Phil and gave them my card for future help.

The next day I received a call from them telling me that Phil had passed away that night. They asked me if I would do the funeral. I agreed. As always, when I got to the funeral I went into the minister's room to reflect on the moment. I promised God years ago that I would never do a funeral without remembering how I felt at my mother's funeral. I would hate for the people to think that my presentation was cold or routine. When my turn came I went to the lectern to begin my presentation (PRESENTATION). I started my funeral message by telling the people that I didn't know Phil but that I wanted to tell them "what I told Phil." Just as I did with the family, I ended my message by saying "Doesn't it make sense to you that you would want to take care of this BEFORE you find yourself in a coma?" Fourteen people opened their hearts to Jesus that day. Funerals are very fruitful for salvations.

It's good that we don't get to decide who goes to heaven and who doesn't. We may never pick people who have AIDS. We may not pick people who have wasted their entire lives without Jesus and at the last minute get saved. I must remember the thief on the cross who had a "death bed" experience, having

71

spent his life pursuing ill gotten gain. It is very good that we are not the judge of such things.

There is still one obvious question to ask here, "Doesn't it make sense to you that you would want to take care of this BEFORE you find yourself in a coma?" Waiting is a dangerous game.

"God didn't and doesn't wait for us to get ready." Unknown

High Tech Evangelism

ﮩﮩﮩ

"There was a time when nails were high-tech. There was a time when people had to be told how to use a telephone. Technology is just a tool. People use tools to improve their lives." - Tom Clancy

One day while sitting in my office, I got very bored. I turned to the computer but there are only so many articles that one can read. I had heard of chat rooms but knew nothing about them. I saw the word "chat" on my computer screen and clicked on it to see what would happen. Most of the things that I had heard about chat rooms were bad. Predators lurk there. People pretending to be someone else frequent such places to do mischief. But I was bored so I clicked on chat.

When the window opened I saw categories from which to choose allowing me to decide what subject I would like to approach. I saw "singles," "cancer survivors," "teens," "single moms," and a host of other subjects. One of the categories was "religion and philosophy." Well now! That looked interesting so I clicked on the subject. The screen actually told me how many people were logged in to that room. I thought that it was pretty neat. Now, let's get to some religion and philosophy. To my surprise, neither religion nor philosophy was being discussed in that chat room. I watched for a few minutes to see what people were typing in their discussions. It all seemed to be simple foolishness.

I decided to see if I could stir things up a bit. Let's move the discussion onto a spiritual path I thought. I typed in "Does anybody here love Jesus?" I was quite surprised at the response. Most of the people typed ugly things to me telling me to get lost or leave them alone or something else equally negative. Only two people actually responded positively. One said "yes" and one typed "I pray to him all of the time." After a little thought, I typed "Did you know that there are rules to prayer?" There were more negative responses but one said "What rules?" Ah ha! I had one hooked.

The next thing that I typed was in answer to the question "What rules?" I typed "what is the first line of the Lord's prayer?" The response came back "Our Father who art in Heaven." I said that's the rule. God must be your Heavenly Father. "Tell me more" came the response. Well, this was getting good. I explained that one must BECOME a child of God and that we are not automatically one.

Suddenly the responses began to come to me in red while my answers were in black. What I didn't know was that this person had gone to a private chat room. We continued this for a few minutes when the other people in the chat room figured out the problem. They told me how to go to the private room. I went there and continued the discussion. It didn't take long before I explained to this person how to open their heart to Jesus. I led them in the sinner's prayer (PRESENTATION) via the keyboard. The response came back to me, "I just prayed that prayer and I feel amazing." I too felt amazing but have learned over the years not to place too much credence in feelings. We all respond differently. **The important part is that one truly opens their heart to Jesus.**

At that time I had a toll free number on my phone where I could receive incoming calls free to the other party. I asked this person to call me. The response came a little slower as they pondered the question "Why?" I typed "too much to tell and too slow to type." In a minute the phone rang and I was talking to my new convert. It was a young girl at work on her boss' computer. She was wasting time on the computer when she should have been working. We had a nice talk that day as she told me of things going on in her life. I asked her if I could mail her a book. She agreed. She actually gave me her address (can you believe that?) where I could mail her a book. I did. We had prayer and the visit was over.

Maybe this is an answer for those who are afraid to present the Gospel. This high tech method can keep you anonymous. Perhaps that could be a good first step down the pathway to unbelievable fulfillment, leading people to Jesus. What do you think?

Text message

❦

"Men never do evil so completely and cheerfully as when they do it from religious conviction." BLAISE PASCAL

As a missionary in Portugal I had many great experiences from which to learn. I learned that most Western European people have little regard for the historic religion of that region of the world. Having been under the authority of the old world Catholic Church for centuries, most people have rejected the ideas and authority of that institution. Remember, this is where the Inquisitions took place. Hundreds of thousands of people were murdered by the church. This is where the Crusades took place, when many more were slaughtered. This is where the worst kind of behavior was performed in the name of religion. This is where kings fought popes over power. This is where religions were born protesting the atrocities of the church. This is where "indulgences" for sin were sold permitting one to commit sin so the "church" could profit. It's no wonder France turned atheistic.

It's no wonder that the people were "turned off" by religion in general.

One lady who became a regular at one of the seeker group Bible studies we conducted was a product of the Western Europe religious history. In search of truth she had embraced the "best" of many religions. She attended a Baptist church; she was born and baptized Catholic; she embraced the teachings of Buddha; she followed several far eastern mystics. She was like Heinz 57 sauce with many different ingredients included. On several occasions, I schemed to get her alone so that I could talk to her privately about her salvation. I had some serious doubts about it.

My wife and I invited her to our apartment one day for a nice leisurely lunch. After lunch we sat in our living room and had a nice chat. I asked her to tell me about her spiritual journey (PRESENTATION). She started at her childhood being born into a Catholic family. She told me about her involvement in that church even performing the duties as a youth leader. She told me about her Eastern influence and her interest in Buddha. She was enamored by people with high education or a big following. She reminded me of the church of Ephesus where they tried to cover all bases, even erecting a statue to the "unknown god" (Acts 17:23).

After about 20 minutes of listening to her story I couldn't take it anymore. I recognized that I must make some kind of confrontation against her scattered religious thoughts. I don't like confrontation but knew that it was necessary in this case. I told her that I had been listening for something special in her talk and that something was missing. I said that I was listening for the name Jesus in her discussion. Well, she got indignant. Of course Jesus was a part of her religious experience. I spent some time telling her that it is very possible to know ABOUT Jesus but not KNOW Jesus. It took a lot of convincing. At one point she seemed to wander off mentally and began to mumble "Is it possible?" I decided to let her go and ponder that for a little while. I assured her that we loved her and only wanted the best for her.

She left our home and was gone about 45 minutes when I got a text message. It said "I have been standing at your corner under a tree since I left your home. I have been wondering where I stand with Jesus. TODAY IS THE DAY; I am accepting Jesus as my Savior today." I hope that she got it. Her journey would be very difficult with so much religious baggage. The big challenge for seekers is to filter what they know about religion through the Bible and not the other way around. It's so easy to get that wrong.

What They Said

꿏

Sometimes people will inadvertently say some very profound things. This section gives some statements or questions that I have heard over the years that have influenced me. It's funny what we remember during simple life experiences.

Can I pray for you?

One day while visiting with a partner, we encountered a group of six or eight young adults sitting on the porch at a condo complex. I gave them all Gospel tracts and waited to see who showed interest. Only one young man showed interest. I cut him out of the group by saying, "Let's step over hear into my office." It was another porch about 25 feet away, but it got us away from the group. My partner was left with the group to give me some uninterrupted time with my new friend. He listened to my presentation intently and was very easily led to Jesus. At the end of my prayer he asked me, "Can I pray for you?" His question is remarkable to me until this very day (over 30 years later). I have never had anyone make that offer before. He prayed that God would bless me and he thanked God for sending me to him on that day. I guess that he could see the value of my visit. Pretty cool!

I can find it

While visiting a first time visitor to the church, we met the young man in his driveway. It was one of those beautiful fall days in Michigan with brightly colored leaves all over the ground. I can still smell the unmistakable fall air. I asked the young man if he died today would he go to heaven. He responded "no, but I'm working on it." I asked him what he meant by that and he replied that he was reading the Bible through, trying to find the answer to that question. I told him that I could help him find the solution to his inquiry but he refused saying, "I can find it." Well that was new to me. Never before had anyone said such a thing to me. Not to be deterred, I asked him what if a truck ran him over before he could find the answer. That made sense to him so I shared the plan of salvation with him. When I got to Romans 3:10 (PRESENTATION) he said, "You mean if I bow my head and ask Jesus to save me He will?" I responded yes. Quickly, he bowed his head and began mouthing a prayer. It stunned me and I said "Wait." Then I couldn't think of a good reason for him to wait. I thought that he had to do it MY way, but of course he didn't. He prayed and asked Jesus to save him WITHOUT my help. The nerve!

My friends gave it to me

As pastors know, many different life situations come up within the church that requires intervention. One young woman in my church had a husband who was hooked on drugs. He struggled to conquer his habit that was costing him *everything* on many levels. I remember driving around to some of his haunts, looking for him when he would go on a drug junket. One day when he was not high I asked him how this whole thing started. He told me that some friends gave him drugs for the first time. FRIENDS! I doubt it. No friend would do that to another.

Can I pray with my eyes opened?

As a missionary in Portugal I regularly conducted seeker Bible studies (VENUE). The hostess of the Bible study had a niece visiting for the summer. She too attended the Bible study. Early on I isolated her from the group to make some spiritual inquiries of her. I asked her to "tell me of her spiritual journey" (PRESENTATION). She told me about her "religious" upbringing which was devoid of a salvation experience. After presenting the Gospel to her (PRESENTATION), she agreed that she needed Jesus. I asked her to bow her head with me to pray and ask Jesus to become her Savior. She asked me, "Can I pray with my eyes opened?" Well, I couldn't think of a good reason not to pray with her eyes opened. Both of us, with heads UP and eyes OPENED prayed the sinner's prayer. I actually found it distracting. It seems to be better for me to close my eyes. Truly, I think that God is just glad to hear from us.

He's not guilty of number 7

While trying to lead a young couple to the Lord on one occasion, I encountered the world's ONLY perfect person. While discussing the matter of sin, the young man told me that he did not consider himself a sinner. Really! I asked him if he had ever taken something that did not belong to him, even the smallest thing. He said that surely he had even without much evil intent. I began to write on a piece of paper, "You're a THIEF." He thought that was pretty harsh. Perhaps, but it was true. I asked him if he had ever told something that was untrue, even the smallest thing. He agreed that it was unlikely that he been perfect in his truth telling. On the piece of paper I wrote "LIAR." At this point his wife chimed in and said "at least he is not guilty of adultery." I thought a minute and said "Jesus said that if you have thoughts of that in your heart you are guilty." "OK, YOU WIN", he said. I guess the scripture is true "all have sinned" (Romans 3:23).

Say it to my face

During my years as a pastor soul-winning was a "constant" for me and the members of my church. One convert began coming regularly to the church services and seemed to enjoy my preaching. In fact she asked if I had my messages taped because she had an interest in growing faster than she could by attending each week. Even though she came for three services on Sunday and one on Wednesday, she felt that she wanted more. I allowed her to borrow all of my master tapes for sermons that I preached for several years. She took everything to heart as she grew. Actually she took all of my messages personally. After one Sunday morning service she stopped by to shake my hand on the way out of church. I will never forget what she said to me that day: "If you have something to say to me, say it to my face." Apparently she thought that I was preaching directly to her that morning. Isn't it fun watching the Holy Spirit stir the heart of new believers?

Is that all there is to it?

One day, I took my friend Tony with me soul-winning. We had a handful of first time visitor cards to visit that day. On one visit we found a lady at home and entered her house for a brief visit. After asking a couple of diagnostic questions about her eternal destiny, I determined that she needed Jesus to be her Savior. She responded favorably to my invitation to help her open her heart to Jesus and invite Him to be her Savior. We left and got back into the car for the short trip to the next visit. Tony's first words to me after reentering the car were "Is that all there is to it?" He found that soul-winning was not a deep theological matter full of apologetics and doctrinal posturing. It was simply "one beggar telling another where to find a handout." It's just sharing a simple truth that has a profound effect. Today Tony has become a serious soul-winner, even teaching others "this is all there is to it."

This is a good day isn't it?

During my two year mission in Portugal, my task was to try to infiltrate the workplace with the Gospel. I was fortunate to be invited into Lisbon Airport to start a seeker group Bible study in one particular office facility. It is my custom not to invite the participants to accept Jesus until the eighth lesson. I want a slow thoughtful process of understanding while pre-discipling at the same time. In this group there were five seekers who regularly attended. On lesson eight, all five of them bowed their heads and accepted Jesus as their Savior. At the end of the prayer we stayed for a few seconds, doing some introspection. The silence was broken when Joao said, "This is a good day isn't it?" Yes indeed!

I'm just listening

In Portugal we found our way into a business, being invited into the office by a delightful Christian young lady. One of the attendees was Sandra. Sandra was a bit cynical but still came regularly. She told me, "I am only listening." Actually more than once she said that. I tried not to make her uncomfortable by too much inclusion into any discussions that we may have had. She did say that she knew that there was "something" but had not yet called Him God. When we made it to the eighth lesson, I addressed Sandra personally saying "I know that you have a problem believing, do you WANT to believe?" She said that she did but lacked faith. I told her that she reminded me of a man in scripture (BRIDGE STATEMENTS). He came to Jesus and asked Jesus if He could heal his sick son. Jesus said that He could if only the man would believe. The man said that he would believe. Then upon further thought he said that he WANTED to believe. In fact if Jesus would help him, he would believe. Then I asked Sandra "can you say that?" She said that she could. I then said, "Let's tell Jesus that you want His help." We bowed our heads and I crafted a quick "I want to believe" prayer. Little did I know that she would immediately exhibit a transformed life. People at her work place began to say "What happened to Sandra; she looks different?" Apparently she got a good dose of salvation.

I Believe

Even though I was not personally involved in this experience, I love to tell about it. My brother-in-law, Gerland, was out one day in the street handing out tracts and engaging people with the Gospel. A Jewish man came by and was handed a gospel tract. As soon as the man looked at the tract, he handed it back saying "I am Jewish, this does not apply to me." Gerland told the man that he wanted to show him more and the man agreed. Turning to Matthew chapter 1, Gerland showed the Jewish fellow the genealogy of Jesus. As the man read the names of the

Old Testament characters, Abraham, Isaac, Jacob, David, Solomon and others, he said, "Hey, these are my guys. Why are they in your book?" Gerland told him that this is the genealogy of Jesus. Then Gerland turned to Isaiah chapter 53, which is known as a Messianic chapter about the coming Messiah. As they read it together, Gerland asked the man if he knew of anyone in history that came to his people and was despised and rejected. As the man pondered the question the "light" came on in his head and the man suddenly said "I BELIEVE." THAT is the kind of belief spoken of in John 3:16 and Romans 10:9. Is that the kind that you have?

Bridge Statements

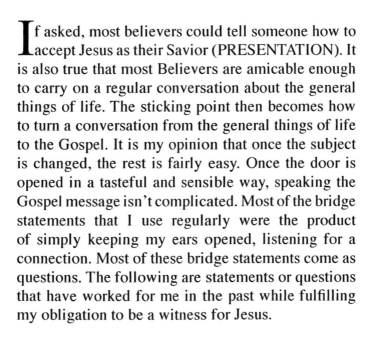

If asked, most believers could tell someone how to accept Jesus as their Savior (PRESENTATION). It is also true that most Believers are amicable enough to carry on a regular conversation about the general things of life. The sticking point then becomes how to turn a conversation from the general things of life to the Gospel. It is my opinion that once the subject is changed, the rest is fairly easy. Once the door is opened in a tasteful and sensible way, speaking the Gospel message isn't complicated. Most of the bridge statements that I use regularly were the product of simply keeping my ears opened, listening for a connection. Most of these bridge statements come as questions. The following are statements or questions that have worked for me in the past while fulfilling my obligation to be a witness for Jesus.

Spiritual journey

During general conversation I find it easy to suddenly shift the conversation by saying, "Hey, I want to hear about your *spiritual* journey. Where are you in that?" It may not get a good response at first but you must press on a bit without acting pushy. You might next ask, "Tell me about your family background from a religious perspective. I love to hear about these things" or "I love to compare stories, they fascinate me." This will get the job done. Of course you must be prepared to steer them to the Gospel. That could easily be done by saying, "Let me tell you about *my* journey."

If you died today

"If you died today do you think that you would go to heaven?" I wish that I had a dollar for every time that I asked that question to someone. Better yet, I wish that I had a dollar for every time *anyone* has asked that question. It has become THE question for this day. Even though I don't think that the question is a great question, I DO think that it will get the conversation turned to spiritual matters. The reason that I don't like the question is that one can give a yes or no answer. I prefer a question that requires a reasoned response. A follow-up question usually accompanies the first one. If the answer is "yes" you will have to ask, "Why do you have that opinion?" The issue is to take the conversation into a spiritual direction.

If you were to stand

Once again, it is a question that turns the conversation spiritual. You could preface things by starting with, "Do you mind if I ask you a spiritual question?" Most people will allow that. The question is, "If you were to stand before God and He asked you, 'Why should I allow you into heaven?' what would you say?'" Be prepared with a follow up statement. "I find the difference responses to that question intriguing." Perhaps you could say, "I had my own ideas about that but I found that they did not match the Bible answer. Someone actually showed me from the Bible the correct answer and it changed my life. Could I share that with you?"

Three legged stool

This one is really easy and simply non-threatening. If you are around people much, sooner or later you will hear someone telling of a problem or crisis in their lives. After being a good listener, it is so easy to ask "may I give you some philosophy?" The answer is always yes. "I have found that life is like a three legged stool. The *first* leg is physical. You must try to take care of yourself physically or your stool will tip over. Things won't go as you would like. The *second* is mental or emotional. You certainly must stay well balanced to avoid problems. The *third* leg is spiritual. This is the one most often neglected. This one allows us to tap into resources that are beyond us. When we need some supernatural help, we can find it. When we need a miracle, it becomes a possibility. When we have no place to turn, we have someplace to turn. This problem you mention is over my head. Why don't we see if we can get God involved in it? What do you think? Before we do that, let's see if we can get God involved in *you*, then we can approach Him together about this problem. Do you want to give it a try?"

What person in crisis would refuse God's help? The Bible allows us to, "Come boldly before the throne of grace, that we may obtain mercy and find grace to help in time of need" Hebrews 4:16. Doesn't this give us a license to bring EVERY problem to God, even the problems of the lost? Maybe these times of "need" are God giving us an opportunity to approach Him and bring the lost to Him.

You're it

If you want to win the lost, how about asking God to bring someone into your path that He wants to bless? Guess what! He will! In fact, He probably already does. Our problem is that we don't have our spiritual antennae up. I remember praying such a prayer one day and sure enough God did His part. My wife and I spent an hour with a brand new person whom we had never met. At one point it was so easy to say, "My wife and I prayed today for God to bring someone to us whom He wants to bless and it looks like *you're the one.* Let's explore this and see what God has in mind. What do you think?" How easy is that? There is nothing threatening about that is there? Try it, you'll like it.

I'm on a spiritual journey

One road block to visiting with another person about spiritual matters is the perception that I may be presenting myself as being "better." The diagnostic questions about one's spiritual life may make one feel that the questioner sees himself as "superior" than the receiver of the question. Such questions may even put a barrier between the two for that same reason. Fear of a situation such as that probably stops many people from approaching spiritual subjects.

In order to avoid this fear or an actual barrier being built one could say something like this, "I am on a spiritual journey to get God to bless my life to the fullest. It occurs to me that you may also have an interest in God blessing your life. Perhaps we could learn together." This works especially well when inviting someone to a Bible study or church service.

Feel, felt, found

Jesus said that "the children of darkness of this generation are wiser than the children of Light" John 16:8. His statement was a bit of a condemnation of believers, lacking wisdom. In any sales training course you might take you will be taught "feel, felt, found." Too bad that the lost world knows how to talk to people, while believers freeze up or say dumb things.

Try this when talking to a lost person. "I know how you feel. I felt the same way, but I have found that ..." It helps you relate to the lost person, putting yourself at the same starting position where *they* are. When leading someone to Jesus, I always give my personal testimony. I always say that someone helped me and I was glad they did. I wanted to accept Jesus but didn't know how. I would have been glad to pray and open my heart to Jesus but needed help. Even if you don't use the exact words "feel, felt, found" use the sentiments of them. Try this, it will help.

You remind me of a person in the Bible

This is a very simple thing to say to anyone that may swing the conversation to spiritual things. More than just a few times, I have used this statement. However in order to use this statement, you must know a little about the Bible and be a good listener, hearing what people say about themselves. The most often used Bible person to which I refer is the man with a sick son found in Mark 9. Read the story and use it often.

Spiritual question

Here is a question that is extremely simple and does not require much forethought: "May I ask you a spiritual question?" Wasn't that easy?

I've been thinking

Often we find ourselves in situations that require us to "think on our feet." Sadly, we may think of the better response the next day. We have a way of wishing that we had handled a witnessing opportunity differently. This is the method that I use to be able to "redeem the time" (Ephesians 5:16). I find that is very affective to go back to the person with whom we were having the conversation and say, "I've been thinking about our conversation the other day." That statement will reopen the door for discussion as well as let the other person know that serious consideration has been made of the dialogue. Try it, you will like it.

Summary

By including some of these "bridge statements" in your vocabulary, much of the anxiety is taken out of having spiritual talks with anyone. Do not treat spiritual talk differently from any other talk. Only YOU think that it is scary proposition. The people to whom you speak don't feel that way. I promise.

Philosophy

❧

Don't get scared, this section will not be too boring. In fact it may be a little fun. Don't turn the page yet.

One advantage of becoming advanced in age is that you have had time to have lots of experiences. This section is about my journey and some of the things that I have learned as well as philosophies that I have formed. These snippets of homespun wisdom will help you on your path to become a strong personal soul-winner.

Swswsw

What? Yep, that's what I said, swswsw. It stands for <u>some will, some won't, so what</u>. One sure fire thing that I have learned is that not everyone will buy into every idea. Of course as we present the Gospel, not everyone will want to pursue accepting Jesus as their Savior. In fact, this is a spiritual issue and theologically one cannot necessarily pick the time when they will accept Jesus. We are taught in scripture by

Jesus that one cannot be saved unless "the Father draws him" (John 6:44). Since that's the case, we can never know whom God is drawing. Therefore, you should not take it personally if your presentation is not accepted. Swswsw. That brings us to the "next" philosophy.

Next

When I fail to win someone to Jesus, I resort to using my favorite four letter word "NEXT." In fact that word works whenever I am unsuccessful in anything. Even the best baseball hitter in modern baseball history only hit 4 out of 10. Ty Cobb was immortalized with a .409 batting average. He is considered a national hero. I consider each failure to win someone as putting me one step closer to the one who will be gloriously saved. I look forward to that awesome experience. It is so much fun. That's why I say "NEXT."

My entire life God has been preparing me for this moment.

It took me 60 years to make that statement. During my life I have been in situations where I wondered out loud "WHY." I spent 10 years trying to make a living doing straight commission sales of insurance and investment products. <u>I hated it</u>! All I wanted to do was serve God. I couldn't imagine why God would put me through that. Then one day while serving as a missionary in Portugal, trying to get into the workplace, I realized that some of the approaches that I used in sales were working for me in Portugal. Some of the sales training that I received actually helped me to succeed in my ministry effort there. Like a lightning bolt out of the blue, I made my statement, "My entire life God has been preparing me for this moment."

That statement was true ten years ago and will be true ten years from now. Do you realize how liberating it is to be able to say that? It will keep you from becoming depressed when you can't figure out a certain phase of your life. <u>How smart is God!</u>

Who's in charge and who gets the credit?

I have reduced the world down to that simple question. I think that the entire world revolves around it. It rules politics, governments, international relations, organizations, churches, and families. How much better would the world be if people did NOT vie for power or credit? What if it didn't matter who got credit for the right opinion? What if we were able to suppress the idea of "opinion"? Would our country be better if the politicians were only interested in the well-being of the country? Could spreading the Gospel be better served without denominations? What if all Christians obeyed Jesus' new commandment to "love one another"? If Jesus came to your city and called all believers to meet in the largest stadium in your city, who would come? Would everyone want to know who was sponsoring the event? Would your marriage be better if you didn't struggle with that question? ***Do you get it?*** Let's just yield to the leading of the Holy Spirit and forget the rest.

Prophet without honor

This is important! Jesus said in John 4:44 "a prophet has no honor in his own country." Since we are known by our context, it is likely that we have less spiritual influence among our own friends than an outsider would. Therefore, unless you are known as a Bible student, preacher, Bible teacher or professional minister, it is best to get some help with your ***own*** circle of friends. By introducing them to an "expert," it is more likely that they will listen and be won to Jesus.

An expert

It has been said that an expert is someone that no one knows, who has a briefcase. That is intended to be funny but it is all too true. People will drive halfway across town and pay $100 to hear an expert talk on a special subject. Since we all can move outside of our own circle of friends, we have the potential of being perceived as an expert. This may be the reason why people feel more comfortable going halfway around the world on a mission trip than going across the street to win somebody. It has been said "in the land of the blind, a one-eyed man is king." Most of us know enough Gospel to save the whole world. To the vast majority of the lost world, we are experts.

Religion

Religion is not an invention of God. Religion *is* the "man-made" set of rules, ideas, dogmas, rituals, do's, don'ts, and practices. All religions make the same claim: they are right and everyone else is wrong. We all know that can't be true. Actually, it is my feeling that religion is my enemy. It becomes a barrier between us and God. I am not a fan of religion. I think that many people who would like to know God and build a relationship with Him are somewhat stymied by religion.

I actually think that man's natural desire for God most often ends up stuck on religion. How else can you explain the myriad of religions in the world? On a quest to find peace and contentment, people are drawn to religion because it seems spiritual. Since Satan is the "father of lies" (John 8:44), it stands to reason that he is the chief inspiration for religion. I have often said that if I were Satan I would fill the world with religion.

While a missionary in Portugal, I was often asked what religion I was. I only answered that question once by saying that I was a Christian. In Western Europe that automatically means Catholic. I am not Catholic but that was the assumption that was made about me. In Western Europe Catholicism is broadly rejected. Almost everyone has been baptized Catholic but that is where they stop. Thousands of Catholic churches are empty. Priests are angry. Only the very old or the stubbornly traditional still embrace old world Catholicism. Most people in Western Europe are disappointed in their religion. Of necessity, I learned to say, "Labels are very confusing. Let's just say that I am a follower of Jesus and that I believe the Bible." It does me no good letting people put me into a labeled box. Even their perception of what they think my label means is a stumbling-block.

If a person was to Google "Christianity" they could assume anything that they like about me. Christianity has a very bad history, depending on what you read about it. Such bad history is the reason that the Muslims hate Christians. When the word "Christian" was first used in Acts 11:26, it was meant as slander. ***Religion is no friend to a soul-winner.***

Hell number two

For those of you who are afraid to share their faith for fear of driving people away. Where would you drive them to "hell number two?" Lost people won't get more lost. They need help whether they know it or not. Surely you can find a tasteful way to say "I'm concerned." (BRIDGE STATEMENTS) Every person should at least have the right to say "NO" to the Gospel. Saying *nothing* deprives a person of that chance.

Comfort

Does sharing your faith make you uncomfortable? Is your comfort the main issue? Was Jesus comfortable on the cross? **Get over it!** I actually think that God always wants us stretching just a bit beyond our comfort level. That's called growth. I remember the very first time that I spoke from the pulpit. **Wow! How scary!** I was only in the pulpit for one minute making an announcement. I thought that I would die. My pant legs actually shook from my knees knocking. I could have said that speaking from the pulpit was not in my comfort zone. I had a similar experience the first time that I shared my faith. The spiritual life has nothing to do with your comfort.

Time and eternity

One day while serving as a systems analyst in county government, I was watching the computer printer print paychecks for the entire county. It was my job to oversee the payroll system for the county. As I watched the checks fly by week in and week out, I was struck with the thought that life can be rather boring. Is this all there is? Living for the next paycheck? God was dealing with me about my own personal priorities. I began to try to measure time versus eternity. It didn't take me long to realize that the best investment of my time was in those things that lasted for eternity. Why spend my life focused on things that pass away? I made the decision to focus on those things that last for eternity.

God designed life for us to need Him

In my experience, God designed life so that sooner or later, we would need Him. If He is "an ever present help in time of need" (Hebrews 4), then the time of need is when we can expect to find Him. It seems, therefore, that the time of need is when He is most readily available to the "lost." The question becomes then, "Was the time of need by His design?" I DO know that God loves dependency. He loves it when we include Him in our lives. I think that we can see God at work during the time when we need Him the most. If we never needed Him, why would we seek Him? **Are you getting this?** The point is, when we see a person in need, it is an opened door for us to introduce the ultimate fix, Jesus.

I've always been a believer

I am struck by the number of people who tell me that they have always believed. They feel that since they have been brought up in a certain religion that "believing" is automatic. That mind-set ignores the "born again" teaching of Jesus in John chapter 3. When a person accepts Jesus as their Savior, the spirit of God enters them. A miracle is performed as a person is literally born into the family of God. Knowing about Jesus for all of your life does not substitute for this eternal transaction with God.

Theologically 33 things happen at the moment of salvation. We are, become or gain: Forgiven, a Child of God, Having access to God, Reconciled, Justified, Placed "in Christ", Acceptable to God, Heavenly citizenship, Of the Family and Household of God, In the Fellowship of the Saints, Within the "Much More" Care of God, Glorified, A Heavenly Association, On the Rock, Jesus Christ, A Part in the Eternal

Plan of God, Redeemed, A Living Relationship with God, Free From the Law, Adoption, Brought Near, Delivered From the Power of Darkness, Entrance Into a New Kingdom, A Gift From God the Father of Christ, Circumcised in Christ, Members of a Royal and Holy Priesthood, A Chosen Generation, A Holy Nation and A Peculiar People, His Inheritance, The Inheritance of the Saints, Light in the Lord, United to the Father, Son and Holy Spirit, Blessed with the First-Fruits of the Holy Spirit, Complete in Him, Possessing Every Spiritual Blessing. WOW, that's like drinking from a fire hose.

Since these things happen instantaneously how could "they" have always believed. That thinking does not allow for the miracle of the new birth.

Intentionality

Life is complicated. We can get so wrapped up in it that we never pay attention to what's important. We spend so much time on the temporary that we almost ignore the eternal. The Lord Jesus thought so much about eternal matters that He died on the cross to help us gain eternal life. That is important. As a bonus, we also get to have Him help us in this life.

If we want to be effective in that for which Jesus died, we must fix our minds on "things that are above." It is unlikely that we will ever think about personal evangelism unless we do it on purpose. You must decide on a venue. You must develop a presentation. You must train your mind to think in bridge statements. You must develop a philosophy that creates an evangelist mindset. You must see people as people who once did not exist but will always exist somewhere. You must become accomplished in sharing your own testimony.

Jewish Conversions

Some very good scripture to use while witnessing to a Jew is as follows:

Matthew 1 gives the genealogy of Messiah linking Jesus to Old Testament Scripture.

Psalm 22 is a Psalm about the Messiah and gives details about the crucifixion.

Isaiah 53 is also a Messianic chapter that shows the rejection of Messiah.

Jeremiah 31:31 talks about God providing a New Covenant for the Jews.

In Matthew 26:28, Jesus refers back to that prophecy announcing its fulfillment.

Daniel 9:24-27 shows Messiah dying *before* the destruction of Jerusalem in 70 A.D.

Linking these verses together will surely help a seeking Jew to find Messiah.

Presentation

꧁꧂

As an associate pastor, my job was to ensure that all first time visitors were visited *and* that an aggressive outreach program was implemented. It made sense to me that all people representing the church should be competent to present the gospel. As a matter of procedure, we began a soul-winning class to ensure that those making follow-up visits could make a sensible presentation of the Gospel. Can you do that?

One day, while on a training visit, I decided to put my trainee into the fray without much notice. I actually knocked on the door and then pushed the trainee up to the door and said, "It's your turn." Wow! Was that enlightening! Even though he had studied the presentation and had appropriately marked his Bible, he suddenly became a fumble bum. As the man of the house answered the door, my trainee began to try to talk. He did so badly that he couldn't identify the top of his testament. He had a difficult time saying anything that made sense.

For your instruction, there are several things that you can do or learn to make the Gospel understandable to all.

Mark your Bible

I have a new testament that I have been using for over 30 years. I marked that Bible when I first bought it to reflect the "Romans Road." The Romans Road is simply a method of presenting the Gospel using the book of Romans. Since the Bible is all about the story of redemption, one could use many other passages to present enough Gospel to win the entire world. For this explanation I will use the Romans Road.

- Starting at Romans 3:10 write the reference for the next verse next to Romans 3:10 in your Bible or New Testament.
- The reference to write next to Romans 3:10 is Romans 3:23.
- At Romans 3:23 write Romans 6:23a.
- At Romans 6:23 write Revelations 21:8.
- At Revelations 21:8 write Romans 5:8.
- At Romans 5:8 write Romans 6:23b.
- At Romans 6:23 write Romans 10:9.
- At Romans 10:9 write Romans 10:13.

I will explain how to use them in the next section. By writing these references next to each verse, the only reference that you need to remember is Romans 3:10. If you can remember Romans 3:10, you can get started with your presentation and know where to go from there.

Make clear points

The points that need to be made using the Romans Road are:

1. We are all sinners, and so are you. (Romans 3:10 and Romans 3:23)
2. There is a price tag for sin - death. (Romans 6:23a and Revelation 21:8)
3. Jesus paid the price for us on the cross. (Romans 5:8)
4. By "believing" He will become our Savior. (Romans 10:9)
5. Tell Him that you are "believing." (Romans 10:13)

It is not enough to simply read the verses. You must tell what point you are making. Tell the listener before you read the verse and tell them *again* after you have read the verse. ***Make the point.***

Watch transitional statements

I find that the statements that make the presentation understandable are the transitional statements. The statements that I use go something like this:

There are four things that you must believe in order to make the connection with God. First we must believe that we have a need.

1. We are all sinners, and so are you. (Romans 3:10 and Romans 3:23)

   Not only are we sinners but there is a price tag on sin.

2. There is a price tag for sin, death. (Romans 6:23a and Revelation 21:8)

   That's the bad news. Now let's hear the good news.

3. Jesus paid the price for us on the cross. (Romans 5:8)

   If Jesus paid for the sins of the entire world, then who goes to heaven and who doesn't? Religion has many answers to that question. Let's ignore what religion says and find out what God says.

4. By "believing" He will become our Savior. (Romans 10:9)

   If you can believe this in your heart then let's tell it to Jesus.

5. Tell Him that you are "believing." (Romans 10:13)

Make the presentation

In this section I will try to give the Gospel presentation as close to realistic as I can. I personally spend some time trying to "make nice." It is important for me to be a regular guy and be liked by the listener. I also feel strongly that my presentation should not seem "canned." I promise that it IS "canned" but practiced well enough so as not to SOUND canned. I will call my listener Joe.

Here we go.

Joe, there are four things that a person must believe in order to make a connection with God. When I say "believe" I will qualify that in a minute. I'm actually talking about a very serious and sincere kind of belief.

The first thing that you must believe is that we have a need. One usually can't be helped until they admit that they need help. The Bible tells us in Romans 3:10 that "there is none righteous no not one." Righteous means in right standing with God at all times and the Bible tells us that no one is like that. In fact the Bible goes on to say in Romans 3:23 that "all have sinned and come short of the glory of God." Sins are those short-comings that we all have that violate the heart and righteousness of God. Simply put, we don't measure up to God's standard. Therefore we must acknowledge that we are sinners.

I'm a sinner, you're a sinner, we are all sinners. Do you agree with that?

The next thing that we must believe is that there is a penalty for sin. In Romans 6:23(a) we are told that "the wages of sin is death." It places a price tag on sin. We all understand wages don't we? Wages are something that we earn. For sin we earn death. But death is more encompassing than we generally think. In Revelation 21:8 we are told about the "second death." The first death is when the body dies and the second death is when the soul dies forever in the "lake of fire." For simplicity let's just call this hell. So the full price for sin is death and death in hell. That doesn't sound like a place where I would like to go. How about you? Now that's the bad news.

Let's see if we can find some good news. In Romans 5:8 we are told "but God commended His love to us in that when we were yet sinners, Christ died for us." So God, knowing that we were under the penalty of death because of sin, sent His Son Jesus to died for us. He died in our place. He died instead of us.

For me that provokes a question. If Christ died for the sins of the entire world, then who goes to heaven and who doesn't? Religion has much to say about that. In fact every religion tries to approach that question. The problem with religion is that is it manmade. How can *man* tell us the way to God? Shouldn't we be listening to God on this matter? Let's see what God says through his word.

In Romans 6:23(b) it says "the gift of God is eternal life through Jesus Christ the Lord." It tells us that God wants to give us something called "eternal life." Here we must understand about the gift. How does one get a gift? A gift is something purchased by someone and offered to another. In order for us to get it we must make a choice. Do I want it or not? Here is the choice, accept the gift of God, eternal life, or reject it and go to hell. Which way would you choose? I choose eternal life, how about you? But how do I receive this gift? What are the mechanics of actually receiving this gift?

In Romans 10:9 we are told "that if you will confess with your mouth the Lord Jesus and believe in your heart that God has raised Him from the dead, you will be saved." It seems to me that we **must** understand what this verse means. Let's look at it phrase by phrase.

First, "if we confess with our mouth the Lord Jesus." This tells us *in whom* to believe. Do you believe that Jesus is the Son of God? Say it. (most all responses are YES) That puts you automatically in the minority. Most of the world will not say that.

Second, "and believe in your heart." That qualifies the *kind* of belief that God requires. We must believe more strongly than a mere surface belief; it must be heartfelt sincerity.

Third, "that God has raised Him from the dead." This tells us *what* to believe about Jesus. God has raised Him from the dead. It tells us that Jesus conquered death. What is our problem? The wages of sin is "death." This scripture tells us where we can go to solve that huge problem. We can take it to the only one who has demonstrated the ability of over-come death, Jesus.

Fourth, "you will be saved." This tells us the *results* of our belief. We will be saved. That's why Jesus is the Savior, one who saves us from something. In this case He saves us from the penalty of sin, which is death, death in hell.

That's what we all want. To have a Savior who can help us with this awful condition and help us make the ultimate connection with God. Jesus is the Savior. Does that make since?

Since this is the only logical choice, we must take our choice to Jesus and tell Him. Romans 10:13 tells us "whosoever shall call upon the name of the Lord, shall be saved." It up to us to take our decision to Him and tell Him that we "believe" and that we accept Him, trusting Him to be our Savior.

This is my basic presentation using the Romans Road. I have used this presentation to win several thousand people to Jesus. This is NOT the only way to present the Gospel, but this one has worked over and over again for me. BUT fishing is only fishing when we gather the fish.

Give your testimony

I always give my testimony at this point. My testimony helps the listener to relate to me, what I did and the decisions that I made. Here is the testimony that I use to relate to the listener:

Here is what happened to me. I went to a Bible study group to be with a girl. Little did I know that the material presented would make sense to me. I expressed interest in learning more, and a man took me aside to share with me. He explained these same things to me that I have explained to you. He showed me from the Bible that I was a sinner. That was not news to me. I knew of my own mischievous nature. He showed me the penalty for sin. I didn't like that much but there it was in the Bible. He told me that Jesus died me for on the cross. I was amazed but grateful. He showed me that if I would believe in Jesus that He would be my Savior. It made sense to me and I wanted to do it. Then he asked me a question. He asked, "Do you want to go to Heaven when you die?" I have thought of that question many times since. He did not ask me what religion I wanted to be. He didn't ask me if I wanted to go to church. Instead he asked me about my eternal destiny. I answered YES. Then he asked, "Could I pray for you?" I couldn't see any reason to say no. Then he said that he would stop in the middle of his prayer and help me to "call on the Lord" asking Him to save me. I was glad that he offered. I wanted to but didn't know what to say.

We bowed our heads and prayed and he helped me to tell Jesus that I wanted Him to save me. When it was over I looked around expecting something to be different. Nothing was. Everything looked to same to me. I thought surely something should change. It took me some weeks or months to realize that there *was* a change but that it was INSIDE ME. My heart had changed. I have never been sorry that I accepted Jesus as my Savior. I could never have imagined the pathway it would put me on. It has been an amazing journey.

Assume the best

Is presenting the Gospel any different from any other presentation which asks for a decision? People are generally fearful about making decisions about anything. Even though this is the greatest decision they will ever make, it may be the easiest. Don't assume that they need to think about it. Don't assume that they must weigh the issues. We already know that they should accept Jesus. We know that there is no down side to it. JUST MOVE AHEAD AND LEAD THEM TO JESUS.

Throughout the presentation we have been asking for little agreements on each sub issue. The prospect does not need much more convincing at this point. Too much convincing may talk them out of it. Don't try to talk them out of making the big decision. Assume the best!

Draw the net

After making my presentation and after giving my testimony, it is time to draw the net. Drawing the net is a fishing term where the fish are actually collected in the net and pulled into the boat. Since we are "fishing for men" drawing the net is an applicable term.

This is when I say,
"May I ask you the same question that was asked of me?" (always answered yes)
"Do you want to go to heaven?" (yes)
"Then let me make the same offer that was made to me; may I pray for you?" (yes)
"I will stop in the middle of my prayer and lead you in a simple prayer helping you ask Jesus to be your savior." (don't wait for a response)
"Remember, prayer must be from a sincere heart. The best you can, try to be sincere."
"Let's bow our heads and pray."

Lead in prayer

"Dear Jesus. Thank you for dying on the cross for us. Thank you also for Joe's interest in connecting with you. Please help him today to be sincere when he asks You to save him." Now Joe, with our heads bowed and eyes closed repeat this prayer with me and be as sincere as you can. "Dear Lord Jesus, I know that I'm a sinner." .... "I'm sorry for my sin." .... "The best I know how, I accept Jesus as my Savior." .... "I know that I can't save myself." .... "So I'm trusting Jesus as my Savior." .... "I need you in my heart." .... "I need you in my life." .... "I need you in my family." .... "Please be my Savior." .... "In the name of Jesus, amen."

The birthing room

I was in the delivery room when both of my children were born. Each time I found myself weeping. I can't really tell you why but I was weeping. Perhaps it was the idea that one more person came out of the room than went in. Perhaps it was the miracle of birth. Perhaps it was in gratitude that everyone survived the experience. Maybe it was just relief. It could have been joy over one more tax deduction. **Who knows!** I can only say that it was an amazing experience.

When someone opens his heart to Jesus, it is a similar experience. New life has been given. It is greater than physical life. It is a life that will live forever. It is a life that will meet you in heaven. It is a life that will reach fulfillment here on the earth as well as final fulfillment in heaven. It will put a person and possibly a family onto the path that God intended for us all. It is the new birth spoken of in John 3. *It is a miracle.*

Venue

꒰ঌ꒱

If a believer in Jesus determines to be a true "witness" (Acts 1:8), he must realize that not many people will come to him asking about Jesus. Only one time in my Christian experience has a person ever approached me about salvation. "In the day" it was well known that members of the church where I was active were openly sharing their faith. An attendant at the gas station I frequented actually came up to me asking to be saved. It didn't take long to explain how it works. It was obvious that he had been considering the matter and that he already knew what he needed. He easily opened his heart to Jesus. ONE TIME IN 38 YEARS! Statistically it never happens. It is therefore incumbent upon the believer to find a venue to share his faith.

I have met some Christians who actively testify routinely in their daily lives. Some have built into their regular conversation lingo that includes spiritual talk. By using words that are spiritual in nature, a door is opened for others to ask questions or to become curious about spiritual matters. Why can't we refer to our spiritual journey, our misguided past, our newfound faith, our dependence on God, our relationship with Jesus, our reliance on Biblical principles? Being overt in our spirituality will certainly keep us from being undercover. I think that it will create "low hanging fruit" - people who watch us and wonder about what makes us tick. However, it is my opinion that generally *most Christians don't talk like that.*

I feel that a motivated believer, interested in winning the lost, should find or create a venue where their faith can be shared regularly. In fact, if we *don't* find a venue, we are not likely to actively share our faith. Listed below are some very deliberate venues for bringing others to faith in Jesus. I have used them all with great success.

Door-to-door (door-to-door boots / Christmas vacation)

I heard a pastor say recently that the day for door-to-door soul-winning is over. I reject such an idea. I DO acknowledge that door-to-door is very hard core witnessing and not for the faint of heart. I DO NOT, however, think that it is dead. In fact Jehovah's Witnesses still do it fearlessly. There ARE several nuances that I have learned while practicing door-to-door witnessing.

1. *Most people are polite.* I have been patronized, dismissed and challenged but have never encountered anger, loudness or violence while going door-

to-door. At worst, I have been rejected. However, one day while visiting door-to-door in an apartment building in inner city Detroit, my brother-in-law Gerland and I had a bad experience. We knocked on a door and a young woman opened the door and said "get lost." She then closed the door. Well, that was enough for me so I began to walk away. Gerland however said "that wasn't very nice" and he knocked on the door again. The young woman came to the door again and repeated her statement. This time she slammed the door loudly. Again I started away when Gerland said again "that was really rude" and he knocked on the door again. This time a man came to the door with an ax handle in his hand. I *knew* that I was ready to leave! Gerland, however, felt that he should try to engage him in a conversation. SLAM WENT THE DOOR! Finally Gerland realized that this would not bear fruit and we left. WHEW! That experience was BOTH of the times that the door was slammed in my face while doing door-to-door soul-winning. It probably could have been avoided. What do you think? Incidentally, I still have never gone door-to-door WITHOUT someone accepting Jesus. It is ALWAYS fruitful.

2. *You must develop a script.* It is very difficult thinking on your feet under a pressure situation. You must predetermine what your opening statement will be and rehearse it. I have found that you have about five seconds to make a case for being given another five seconds. You must quickly

identify yourself and tell what you are doing on their porch. Perhaps you could hand out a brochure or a pamphlet. Perhaps it could advertise the church or some benefit to the resident of the home. Most people want to know only one thing while deciding to entertain an unexpected guest, "WIIFM" (what's in it for me). A perceived need must be presented such as "we are just inviting people to church" (perhaps they have a felt need to attend church). I developed a script that mentioned an invitation to church but quickly shifted to the gospel. By handing them a tract with the church info on the front I could then say, "By the way, inside it tells you how you can know for sure that you are going to heaven when you die, I guess we all care about that don't we?" Their reaction to that question would allow me to know how to proceed. If they responded positively to that question, I would withdraw the tract and say "I'm somewhat of a specialist in that area. May I share with you how that works?" The response lets you know where to go from there. *A predetermined script is an absolute requirement.*

3. ***You must be thick skinned.*** The easiest way to do that is not to take anything personally. The people you may encounter don't know you. If they *knew* you they would probably learn to like you. You **personally** will not be rejected. Your visit may be. Perhaps you have interrupted something. Remember, your visit is unexpected. Simply be nice, follow the script and don't expect to be

invited into every home you visit. It just won't happen. In fact, you may only find one in ten people who will welcome your visit. Just remember that Jesus Himself spent three years in public ministry, demonstrating miraculous power, feeding and healing thousands, even raising the dead, but only three hundred people were found in the upper room on the day of Pentecost. Honestly, going door-to-door is exhausting emotionally. Most people can't divorce themselves from the rejection.

4. *You will make some lifelong friends.* From door-to-door soul-winning, I have seen hundreds saved, lives transformed, families restored, converts discipled, and even ministers produced. I've seen hundreds get started in church and hundreds baptized. One family I encountered and won to Jesus became regular in church and began to call themselves "Charlie's Angels" in my honor. One of my best friends in the world today came from door-to-door visitation.

5. *It is empowering.* If you ever do door-to-door soul-winning for any length of time, it will lift your confidence level through the roof. Your bold-ness quotient will forever be raised. It will make witnessing to your friends and family almost easy, having succeeded at *hard core evangelism.*

Bus ministry teaching/Sunday school teachers

Aggressive bus ministries do not still exist as they did in the 70's. I'm sure that some churches still offer to pick up people for church but the aggressive evangelistic ministry where people are receiving Jesus by the droves does not exist today. However, I am convinced that the principles used then can still be used now through the Sunday school. I think that any Sunday school teacher can pick up neighborhood kids in his car and take them to church. *Anyone* can win a fifth grader to Jesus. Maybe it's not as challenging as winning a drug dealer, but it can have as big an impact in the cosmic scheme of things. In fact it may prevent a child from turning *into* a drug dealer.

If a child is entrusted to a neighbor (you) to be taken to Sunday school, it creates an open door to win the parents. Simply by dropping by and telling the parents, "We know that every parent cares what their kids are taught in Sunday school." Entrance can be made into *any* home at *any* time. I did this years ago when I was a bus captain. My wife Jeanette and I used to pick up a hundred kids a week for Sunday school. I would spend all day Saturday out rounding up kids and then we would pick them up on Sunday. On our bus we had a driver, navigator, stewardess, captain and a musician (my wife played the accordion). This was a well oiled machine (INTENTIONALITY). While using information I gathered on Saturday, I would let the navigator know at which homes to stop. The navigator would sit behind the driver and convey the directions. The stewardess would help maintain order on the bus and get information from the new kids. My wife would play the accordion and lead singing. I was free to oversee the entire thing. I enlisted the help of a bus mom on the route to call ahead to get the kids up as the bus was coming. It seems that the parents didn't always care enough to get the children up on Sunday. Hundreds of kids accepted Jesus.

On Tuesday and Thursday evenings I would get a partner and go visit the parents. As I was greeted at the door, I would say, "Hi kids, tonight is for parents." Of course, I knew the parents by then, having picked up their kids for some time. I would tell them, "We know that every parent cares what their kids are taught in Sunday school and tonight we are here to share that with you." We were always let in and always given a hearing. What parent in his right mind would say, "I don't care what you teach my kids"? They were obligated to listen. We discussed some of our methods of teaching, assuring the parents that we only taught the Bible, not religion. We then told them that the main thing that we taught was how to get to heaven when we die. After giving the details of the Gospel, many parents accepted Jesus themselves. Hundreds were saved.

This approach could work at *any time* that a Sunday school teacher decided to work it. Every Sunday school teacher should do this. In fact, you don't even need to be a teacher. Just pick up a neighborhood child and take him to Sunday school.

When the late Jerry Falwell started his ministry while in college, he was given a class of fifth grade boys. In the church where he attended, they didn't have a room where he could meet with his class. In fact they didn't have any fifth grade boys for him to teach. They *did* find him a space in the furnace room where he could teach (don't tell the fire marshall). He began to find fifth grade boys in his neighborhood. After a short while his Sunday school leaders were forced to find a room for him. Not long after that he had 200 fifth grade boys. Can you imagine how many parents he would win through those kids? The rest is history.

It is my opinion that this method is the absolute easiest method of reaching people for Jesus.

Chaplain

Even though not everyone can be a corporate chaplain, I feel that I should mention this as a venue that has been very fruitful for me. I spent five years as a Corporate Chaplain through Corporate Chaplains of America. My task was to see every employee every week to offer any spiritual help that they might need. I actually saw 700 employees every week who worked for 6 different companies. It was not as difficult as it sounds to engage 700 employees. Most of the time, the greeting was a simple, "Hi, how are you doing today? Is everything okay with your family? Can I do anything for you today?" Usually it only took a minute or two for this brief encounter.

Having pledged confidentiality, I was regularly drawn into employees' life issues. It could be anything from illness to marital problems, from drug issues to a family death, from trouble with the law to premarital counseling. It was common to spend only minutes with an employee but just as common to spend a couple of weeks with an individual and his family, trying to solve a problem.

I adopted the idea that a problem was an open door for me to introduce Jesus into the situation. In Hebrews 4:16 we are invited to "come boldly to the throne of grace, that we may obtain mercy and find grace to help in *time of need*." Since that offer is made to us, why should we try to solve "needs" without including Jesus? I found it very easy to bridge (BRIDGE STATEMENTS) from the problem to Jesus. It only seemed natural for me to say, "This problem is over my head; let's see if we can get God involved. But before we do that, let's get God involved in you; then we can approach Him together about this issue." Most people involved in a life conflict are very open to drawing on supernatural power.

As a chaplain I was involved in many weddings and funerals. Both of them were high yield for salvations. Each will be discussed below by itself. It is quite possible to make a tasteful and appropriate presentation of the Gospel during both weddings and funerals. All told, I saw 650 people come to Jesus during my 5 years as a corporate chaplain. Around 150 of the 650 came regularly to Bible studies. It was a good time for evangelism and discipleship.

You may not be able to become a corporate chaplain but some of these evangelistic ideas can be used by anyone who regularly interacts with other people, perhaps at work or in the neighborhood.

Man of peace

Luke 10:5-7 tells us about a man of peace. This person is a help to those trying to follow the Great Commission, evangelizing the world. A man of peace is a person who has some influence and will allow our "soul-winner" the opportunity to interact within that circle. Depending on that person's credibility, many can come to Jesus. There are several ways that I have used the influence of a man of peace in my evangelistic ministry. By the way, there is no reason to limit yourself to one man of peace. At this writing I am working with 12 men of peace. Each one opens up a new horizon for lost people.

1. **New converts** are a great resource for more new converts. In John 4, after her conversion, the "woman at the well" went back into the city testifying, and many of the people of that city believed on Jesus. Years ago, while pastoring, several new converts in my church caught the vision of reaching their friends and families. One lady brought 40 people from her circle all on the same Sunday. Many of them received Jesus that day and others were led to Jesus in their homes on follow-up visits. Another lady convert caught fire for Jesus and ended up serving in the bus ministry.

She was responsible for bringing hundreds to church and to Jesus. One of my stories mentioned earlier in the book was of a man and wife saved during my personal neighborhood visits. They led me to dozens of people who accepted Jesus. *Never underestimate the value of one new convert.*

2. **A business owner** can be an incredible resource for evangelism. If they will let you into their business either to hold Bible studies or to personally visit with employees, people will come to Jesus. It has been my great privilege to serve several businesses as chaplain. Hundreds came to Jesus. In my opinion, Christian business owners have a stewardship responsibility to share the Gospel with their employees. Perhaps the employees have no interest, but should at least be given the opportunity to say NO. The vast majority of the world has never had the blessing of making that choice. It seems to me that a business owner should allow a person to come into their business, offering the opportunity to employees to hear the Gospel. The owner probably shouldn't try overtly to win his employees personally because of the "owner/ employee" relationship. It would be very awkward and may even cause legal issues. As I write this paragraph, I am encouraged to go find a business owner.

3. **A seasoned Christian** can also be a wonderful "man of peace." Unfortunately most Believers do not or will not try to reach their friends and fami-

lies (PHILOSOPHY). They will therefore have
unreached family members, friends or neighbors.
The older a Christian gets the fewer lost friends
he will have. Most seasoned Christians will find
their associations in church and never try to reach
anyone. They grow content and complacent among
the "brethren." They love going to church, prayer
meetings where they pray for sick church or family
members. The closer they get to death themselves
the more conscious they become of their own
mortality and they seem to sink into a pattern of
measuring their lives by how many surgeries they
have had. To me this is a pitiful state. They seem
happy enough but are missing the real joy that God
has for those who partner with Him in reaching
souls for Jesus.

If, however, they get inspired to see the lost
saved, they can put you into a vast pool of lost
people. They probably won't try to win them
themselves but they will cheer for you as you do.
It seems that one should try to come along side
of these folks. They won't take much convincing
but they will need inspiring. If they do sign on to
become a "man of peace" they will find a renewed
zeal and purpose for life. Nothing is more exciting
to me than visiting the nursery where souls are
being born into the Kingdom of God.

4. **A pastor** has more influence than most. He can
   become a true man of peace by hooking you up
   with *all of the above.* I served as a missionary in
   Portugal for two years. One prominent pastor put

me on the map quickly. He was more interested in "Kingdom" work than most. By that, I mean that he could see the value of people being saved and discipled regardless of whether or not the convert came to HIS church. In my opinion, many pastors have an imbalance in their thinking toward their own church *building*. I have even known pastors who would discourage some of their best workers from answering the call to ministry, in order to keep them in their own churches. I certainly understand that kind of thinking but don't subscribe to it.

If you want to win souls, go to your pastor and ask him if he could hook you up with a businessman, new convert or a seasoned Christian with a Kingdom mindset. He will gladly do it.

Bible studies

What if I told you that you can get lost people to come to a Bible study group? Over the past few years I have developed a method of drawing together "seekers" into small study groups. Some of them have been in the workplace and some in neighborhoods. Several philosophical conditions must be met to make it happen.

1. A **host** of a Bible study must NOT teach his own group. Most people are known by their *context* and not by their spiritual journey (PHILOSOPHY). An accountant is not normally known as a Bible teacher. Therefore by enlisting the help of an

"expert" (someone with a briefcase that no one knows) to teach the class, "seekers" are more likely to come. Many people will drive half-way across town and pay $100 to hear an "expert" speak on a certain subject, such as real estate investing. By touting the credentials of the teacher some people will identify with him.

2. **"Low hanging fruit"** will be found somewhere around a believer, assuming the believer is the "right kind." It is impossible to tell what God may be doing in the life of a lost person. At any time a person may be having a personal struggle where they may be searching for answers. The timing may be just right for them to be invited to a Bible study group where they can find out "how to get God to bless their life."

My father was low hanging fruit when he accepted Jesus. He was having a bad summer because he had three teenage sons who kept getting into trouble (I was one of them). My father realized that he needed some help in his life and the timing was right. When presented the option, he accepted Jesus.

Let our serious believers invite friends, family and neighbors (or workplace colleagues) to a Bible study taught by a specialist as mentioned above. The timing will be right for some.

3. **Take your time** getting to the Gospel. I have developed a series of lessons (www.charlesyoungphd.com) that present the story of redemp-

tion in a methodical method. The participant is not given the option of accepting Jesus until the eighth lesson. Almost all of them do. I call this pre-discipleship. By the time the convert is saved they already have developed a custom of meeting together, praying, and reading the Bible in a small group. There is no reason to stop. Groups that I start just keep going.

4. **Don't worry about the results**. It is God's business to draw sinners. We cannot do God's work. Only He can decide who He wants to save at any given moment. If only one person comes to the Bible study, it is enough. The person could be the next Billy Graham.

5. **Don't criticize any particular religion**. During the first lesson I always tell the group that we will not be studying religion. I say that religion is not invented by God. Religion is the "man-made" set of rules, ideas, dogmas, rituals, do's, don'ts, and practices. All religions make the same claim, they are right and everyone else is wrong. We all know that can't be true. Actually, it is my feeling that religion is my enemy. It becomes a barrier between us and God (PHILOSOPHY). While teaching it is better to say "we can go directly to Jesus with our prayers" than to say "you don't need to pray through a priest." The later statement is an attack on some religions. It may be a correct statement but not necessary to say. It will actually be counter-productive.

6. **Follow the new convert's family.** What a thrill to see a person give his heart to Jesus. An equal thrill is to see that person develop an interest in seeing his family become followers of Jesus. A family coming to Jesus completes the family. Anything less leaves the family incomplete. A new convert's zeal for his family and his newfound faith is a powerful tool for evangelism. Use it wisely.

Church visitors

A very easy kind of visit to make is to first-time visitors to church. They have already expressed an interest by attending and they probably have some questions. Some may already be believers and some will be seeking spiritual help.

Years ago I was the visitation director of a fast-growing church in Michigan. We would have as many as 100 first time visitors per week. Most of them were bus ministry people and many of them were drive-in visitors. It was typical for us to have special promotion days which could draw in as many as 200 drive-in visitors on any given Sunday. My task was to see to it that these people were visited on a timely basis. I enlisted the help of some good people who, after some training, did a great job with these follow-up visits. I personally made a large portion of these visits per week. Hundreds of people were led to Jesus during those fruitful days. I learned some tremendous truths during that time that have served me well over the years.

Even though a visitor may already have a church background I never assume that they are saved. So as not to insult, I change the diagnostic questions that I ask a church person. I might ask them, "How long have you been a believer." This is a soft question that does not sound "diagnostic." A follow-up statement could be, "Tell me about that experience, I would love to hear it." It won't take long for you to learn of their salvation or the lack of it. Even if they tell me of a reasonable salvation experience, I might then ask, "Did it take?" meaning did it actually make a difference in your life. I have had some actually tell me "no."

For those people who don't actually have a church from which they are visiting, I might ask, "What is your religious background." That gives me some frame of reference for our discussion. I also like to ask, "What made you come to church now?" This may reveal a need in their lives. Even though I have asked the question, "If you died today would you go to heaven," I don't particularly like it. It seems too intrusive. Over the years I have concluded that the Apostle Paul, after his conversion in Acts 9, may not have answered that question correctly. His issue was not "going to heaven" but instead it was "who is Jesus." When he answered that question correctly from the heart, he was converted. I prefer the question, "How do you stand with God?" It is not a yes or no question and requires some thoughtful answer. If they have been saved, they will tell you. If not they will also tell you.

By the way, I never call ahead before stopping by. In these days of voicemail, you may never get to talk to them anyway. Phoning ahead gives the visitor too many outs from the visit. It also seems most likely that you will get permission to visit a church member from another church but NOT get in to see non-believers. I *always* drop in for the visit and say, "I just took a chance that this would be a good time to stop by; could I take just a minute?"

Funerals

As a pastor, I made it a practice to drop in to several funeral homes in close proximity of my church. I offered my services to perform funerals for those who did not have a pastor. Amazingly, I would do at least one a month. The challenge was to develop a sermon that could be generic enough to work for anyone and tasteful enough to share the Gospel in an unobtrusive way. Listed below are some pertinent thoughts for consideration.

1. **More lost people will come to this event than you could ever get to come to church**. Plus the people who come will be sensitive about death, with questions about destiny and the afterlife. Could you ever get an audience with a more open mindset? *Use this time wisely!*

2. **Religion should not be made an issue**. At a time like this religion is immaterial. In fact the religion of the deceased is immaterial. The only thing that

matters during this sermon is that Jesus is presented as an option determining a person's destiny.

3. **Make nice**. It only takes but a few minutes to speak with family members to get a few anecdotal stories telling of some personal traits of the deceased. These stories make the message a little more personal and your sermon not so sterile.

4. **The following is an outline** that I have used many times. I have always had people respond, accepting Jesus as their Savior. The Gospel *can* be presented without making people feel that you have violated their trust.

FUNERAL GOSPEL

Make nice

Today's purpose Eccl. 7 *(I view this passage as a mandate for those who preach funerals to share the Gospel message)*

[1] A good name *is* better than precious ointment,
And the day of death than the day of one's birth;
[2] Better to go to the house of mourning
Than to go to the house of feasting,
For that *is* the end of all men;
And the living will take *it* to heart.
[3] Sorrow *is* better than laughter,

For by a sad countenance the heart is made better.
[4] The heart of the wise *is* in the house of mourning,
But the heart of fools *is* in the house of mirth.

V 1	**This view assumes that we are entering a sin cursed world at birth and a *sinless* world at death.**
V 2	**This is the end of all men, this is reality.**
V2	**The living will check reality.**
V3	**The attendee's job is to have your heart "made better."**
	The preacher's job is to help with that.
V4	**Only wise people will heed this message.**

Why this death?   Job 14

[1] "Man *who is* born of woman
    is of few days and full of trouble.
[2] He comes forth like a flower and fades away;
    He flees like a shadow and does not continue.
[3] And do you open Your eyes on such a one,
    And bring me to judgment with Yourself?
[4] Who can bring a clean *thing* out of an unclean?

No one!
⁵ Since his days *are* determined,
the number of his months *is* with You;
You have appointed his limits, so that he cannot
pass.
⁶ Look away from him that he may rest,
till like a hired man he finishes his day.
⁷ "For there is hope for a tree,
if it is cut down, that it will sprout again,
And that its tender shoots will not cease.
⁸ Though its root may grow old in the earth,
and its stump may die in the ground,
⁹ *Yet* at the scent of water it will bud
and bring forth branches like a plant.
¹⁰ But man dies and is laid away;
Indeed he breathes his last
and where *is* he?
¹¹ *As* water disappears from the sea,
And a river becomes parched and dries up,
¹² So man lies down and does not rise.
Till the heavens *are* no more,
they will not awake
nor be roused from their sleep.
¹³ "Oh, that You would hide me in the grave,
that You would conceal me until Your wrath
is past,
that You would appoint me a set time, and
remember me!
¹⁴ If a man dies, shall he live *again?*
All the days of my hard service I will wait,
till my change comes.

V1   Can you relate to that?

V2   Sometimes man seems "cut down."

V5   Though he would like more life God says no. Sometimes this is the only answer that makes sense.

V10   (only if you know) Where is he?

V13-14 God has a set time for a resurrection/reunion

(I only read the noted verses.)

In keeping with the deceased's wishes

You said   "He would have liked these flowers."

"He would have liked this suit" music etc.

My view   What would he want NOW?

Having been off in eternity these few days

I know what he would want.

In view of scripture, he would want me to:

"Tell them not to miss heaven"

"Make sure at all costs they go to heaven.

"Tell my family and friends how."

In keeping with his wishes, here it is:

Plan of salvation
Group prayer accepting Jesus (do not do this out loud)
Raise hands as silent testimony "What is the value of *this* death"
Hope   Psm 30:5 "Weeping may endure for a night but joy comes in the morning"
Note be careful not to make much of his destiny if unsure of heaven.
His wishes would be the same either way.

5. **Follow-up**. This is a very difficult issue but needs to be addressed. One thing that I tried was preparing a packet containing a death-sensitive letter, a church brochure and a sermon recording. My purpose was to try to give encouragement as well as a challenge for them to pursue their newfound faith. I invited those who prayed along with me for the first time, accepting Jesus, to stop by and pick up a packet from a certain location (my open briefcase). Every time all of the packets were taken. I *never* had anyone come to church as a result of doing a funeral. I have experienced as many as 60 people respond by raising their hands. It is impossible to know where their spiritual journey took them. God only knows.

Weddings

Weddings draw as many lost people as funerals. The big difference is that the participants do not have eternity on their minds. There is a way, however, to bring out spiritual truths using the wedding as a backdrop for the Gospel. It took me 30 years of ministry to make this connection and I am amazed that I didn't think of this sooner. Once I got this figured out, it has been a great and very tasteful way to present the Gospel. Follow the outline below and the message will become very clear. This presentation is to be used after the vows are exchanged and the wedding party is dismissed. The wedding party should hear this presentation on the evening of the rehearsal because they will not hear it after they have been dismissed after the vows.

Wedding Gospel

May I make a few final comments to you?

What you just witnessed is a wedding. The way it happened is, the groom made a proposal to the bride.
  Will you:
      Be mine
      Change your destiny
      Let me love you unconditionally
      Let me forgive all of your faults
      Change your name
      Change your address
      Let me take care of you all of your life
      Bear my children

The bride then considers the proposal and says *yes.*

They then come to me and we exchange some vows and a new relationship is begun.

What you also have witnessed is a drama. This is the picture God chose to use to show how we make our connection to Him.

Our heavenly bridegroom (Jesus) makes a proposal to us.
(repeat the list.)

We then, as the proposed bride, must make a decision. Should I accept His proposal?

I have always thought it unwise to reject the proposal of God.

If it makes sense to us and we would like to do so, then we accept His proposal.

If you have said to yourself that it makes sense, then we must tell Him.   YES

I'm here to help you exchange some vows with Him.

Let's all bow our heads. Please repeat this prayer with me quietly in your heart.

(an appropriate sinners prayer....+ yes I accept your proposal today)

With our heads still bowed, if you prayed along with me, accepting Jesus today, lift your head and make eye contact with me. I have a final word.

Just like in our marriage today, a lifelong journey has begun with Jesus.

The more you put into this new relationship the more you will get out of it.

It doesn't work well to ignore your spouse and it won't work well ignoring Jesus.

Final prayer

Marriage and pre-marital counseling

During marital and premarital counseling is a perfect time to present the Gospel. I always start in the same way for each. I John 4:7-8 tells us, "Beloved let us love one another for love is of God; and everyone who loves is born of God and knows God. He who does not love does not know God, for God is love."

If a marriage is to be based on love, then we must understand this verse for it seems to be a key concept for a good relationship. As we parse these verses, we must ask "what does this mean?" What kind of love is this talking about? Are we to assume that every person that says "I love you" is born of God? Does every teenager who "falls in love" find peace with God? What's going on here?

At least three different Greek words are used for the word love as taught in the Bible. "Eros" is one of those words. "Eros" is the word from which we derive the word erotic. This kind of love is probably the first attraction that we feel in a male, female relationship. It is a sensual attraction. "Eros" is a gift from God and is a very strong sexual attraction which is almost totally self serving. It is also temporary. This strong attraction creates a chemical high in the brain which can even cause you to lose your moral compass. It can become addictive and often does in some people who focus on it. This kind of love will not support a marital relationship for long. People mature and the sexual attraction diminishes.

Another Greek word is "phileo." This is a brotherly kind of love. In fact this is the word from which the city of Philadelphia gets its name. This brotherly love is at the level of having things in common. Once the initial attraction is made, a couple then finds out if they have "things in common." This causes couples to spend hours learning about each other. This is one big cause of high cell phone bills! Because of its nature, it too is self-serving and somewhat temporary. Interests change over time. This kind of love is also not strong enough to sustain a marital relationship.

The last Greek word is "agape." This love comes from God. When the Bible says "God is love" it is this love that is being spoken of. Since the verse says "Everyone who loves is born of God," it indicates that you cannot even possess this kind of love unless you are born of God. This is the love spoken of by Jesus in John 15 when He says that He has given us a new commandment, that we love one another. Since this is commanded, it can be *obeyed.* It is not something that we "fall" into; it is something that we **choose** to do. This kind of love is different from the two mentioned above, in that we can choose it and it is NOT self serving. It is a choice to serve *others.* This kind of love *will* sustain a marriage because it is not felt but chosen.

During marriage or pre-marital counseling this distinction should be made. Then the question can be asked, "You don't want to cheat your spouse from the best kind of love do you?" Then a discussion about what it means to be "born of God" can ensue. I have actually had a man say to me "I think we need Jesus" after such a discussion. Both man and woman accepted Jesus that day.

Back to the subject of venue.

Regardless of the venue you choose, it is not likely that you will consistently win people to Jesus unless you find a venue where you can serve. Don't worry about being comfortable. It has never been about your comfort. I think that God wants us to always be stretching ourselves. Jesus certainly wasn't comfortable at Calvary.

Let's Get To It

꒰꒱

"The world is a dangerous place to live; not because of the people who are evil, but because of the people who don't do anything about it." - Albert Einstein

Can personal evangelism have a broad effect? I am of the opinion that a life, a home, a family, business, institution and even a nation can be affected by spreading the Gospel. Proverbs 13:34 tells us that, "Righteousness exalts a nation but sin is a reproach to any people." Since righteousness follows salvation, every person trusting Jesus as their Savoir changes the nation little by little. As people "let their light shine before men" (Matthew 5:16), righteousness spreads outwardly.

Do you remember the story of Lot in Sodom and Gomorrah in the Old Testament (Genesis 18 and 19)? God lamented the sinfulness of the city in which Lot chose to live. It was so horrible that the men of the city sought to sodomize two angels that had visited Lot. God decided to destroy those wicked cities and all of their inhabitants. He had made an announce-ment to Abraham that He would destroy Sodom and Gomorrah because of their great sin. Abraham decided to try to make a bargain with God to get Him to spare the cities. Abraham asked God if He would destroy the righteous with the wicked. God told Abraham that if there were 50 righteous people in the city that He would spare it. Abraham began to haggle with God regarding the number of righteous people in the city. They settled on 10. God agreed that if there were 10 righteous people in Sodom that He would spare the city.

Soon Lot was warned by God to flee the city with his family. Lot's sons-in-law thought he was crazy and laughed at him. Apparently God did not find 10 righteous people within the city for He poured out fire and brimstone upon the city immediately after Lot, his wife and two daughters fled. Even though Lot had risen to prominence in that city, he didn't have enough influence with the people of that city to turn them to God. Do you suppose that if Lot had been a soul-winner, 10 righteous people would have been found by God? God would have spared the city if there were 10 "believers" there. Perhaps Lot could have saved the entire city by being a soul-winner. Think about it!

How has your life and Christian walk affected the country in which you live? Have you been obedient to the Lord's command to "Go therefore and make disciples of all nations"? Have you tried to win *anyone* to Jesus? Maybe this will be a turning point in your life. Let's get busy!

About the Author

༺✦༻

Charles O. Young holds several degrees including: a Bachelor in Religious Education, a Master of Ministry, a Doctor of Philosophy in Christian Counseling and a Doctor of Ministry. His history includes having been a senior pastor in the United States and is a Licensed Clinical Christian Counselor. For five years he was a corporate chaplain, winning hundreds of people to Jesus. Dr. Young has taught the Bible in Spain, Portugal, North Africa, Haiti, Mexico, Israel, Kenya, and Ethiopia.

After spending two years as an International Mission Board, SBC missionary in Portugal, he developed the passion to see people, the *world over*, understand and embrace the love of God. It has been his joy to lead several thousand people to Jesus. Today he leads a non-profit organization called "Workplace Paracletes." Its aim is to gather seekers into Bible study groups in the workplace or neighborhoods, leading them to Jesus. (www.workplacefruits.com)

"**D**r. Charles Young is an innovative and authentic evangelist whose insight into the process and people involved in evangelism is unrivaled. His book, like the Gospel, is full of grace and truth."

Sam R. Williams, Ph.D.
Associate Professor of Counseling
Southeastern Baptist Theological Seminary
****

"This book is exceptionally creative and very readable. As you read the real life witnessing stories of Charles Young, you will laugh, cry, be inspired and instructed. Dr. Young offers us innovative ways to engage people while at the same time not "bruising the fruit." In my estimation, this book has the potential to revolutionize our evangelistic effectiveness."

Dr. George A. Thomasson
Senior Associate Pastor
Bell Shoals Baptist Church, Brandon Florida
****

"This book sidesteps the maze of ecclesiastic labels to get to the heart of Christ who came to "seek and save the lost." Some books are meant to be read and shelved and not used, but that's not true of this book of evangelist helps. It is with a burning heart that I commend a book that will capture truth in simple language that speaks to the heart, not just the head."

Dr. Bob Anderson
Special Advisor to the Senior Pastor
Bell Shoals Baptist Church, Brandon Florida
****

"Charles Young has compiled years of experience into a practical guide in which any Christian can not only feel comfortable but bold in engaging friends and strangers with the claims of Christ. Applying the tools and advice in "Charging Hell With a Squirt-gun" will give the reader joy in leading others to faith in Christ and finding soul-winning becoming a compelling life passion."

Jerry Rankin, President
International Missions Board, SBC
****

The "Great Commission" isn't called the "Great Suggestion" and you have shown multiple examples of ways in which anyone can share the Gospel with minimum fear. Your book is a great encouragement and challenge for all of Christ's followers. Thank you for writing this book and sharing your heart.

Ken Boyle
Friend and passionate follower of Jesus